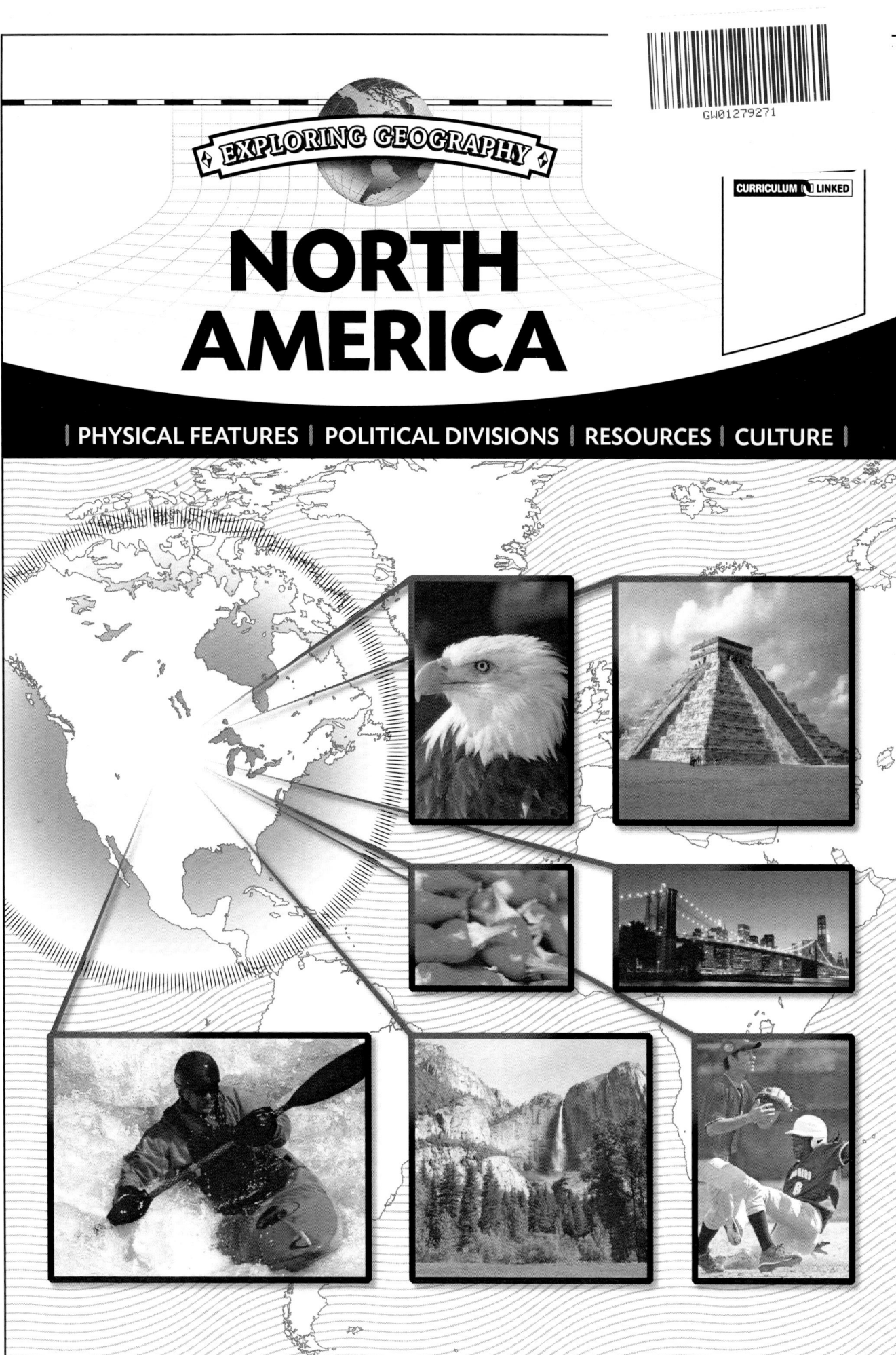

Exploring geography: North America
(Middle/Upper primary)

Published by Prim-Ed Publishing 2013 under licence from Evan-Moor® Educational Publishers

Copyright© 2010 Evan-Moor® Educational Publishers

This version copyright© Prim-Ed Publishing 2013

Revised and reprinted 2016

ISBN 978-1-84654-660-0

PR– 6365

Titles available in this series:
Beginning geography *(Lower/Middle primary)*
Exploring geography: Africa *(Middle/Upper primary)*
Exploring geography: Antarctica *(Middle/Upper primary)*
Exploring geography: Asia *(Middle/Upper primary)*
Exploring geography: Australia & Oceania *(Middle/Upper primary)*
Exploring geography: Europe *(Middle/Upper primary)*
Exploring geography: North America *(Middle/Upper primary)*
Exploring geography: South America *(Middle/Upper primary)*

This master may only be reproduced by the original purchaser for use with their class(es). The publisher prohibits the loaning or onselling of this master for the purposes of reproduction.

Copyright Notice

Blackline masters or copy masters are published and sold with a limited copyright. This copyright allows publishers to provide teachers and schools with a wide range of learning activities without copyright being breached. This limited copyright allows the purchaser to make sufficient copies for use within their own education institution. The copyright is not transferable, nor can it be onsold. Following these instructions is not essential but will ensure that you, as the purchaser, have evidence of legal ownership to the copyright if inspection occurs.

For your added protection in the case of copyright inspection, please complete the form below. Retain this form, the complete original document and the invoice or receipt as proof of purchase.

Name of Purchaser:

_____

Date of Purchase:

_____

Supplier:

_____

School Order# (if applicable):

_____

Signature of Purchaser:

_____

Internet websites

In some cases, websites or specific URLs may be recommended. While these are checked and rechecked at the time of publication, the publisher has no control over any subsequent changes which may be made to webpages. It is *strongly* recommended that the class teacher checks *all* URLs before allowing pupils to access them.

View all pages online   **Website:** www.prim-ed.com

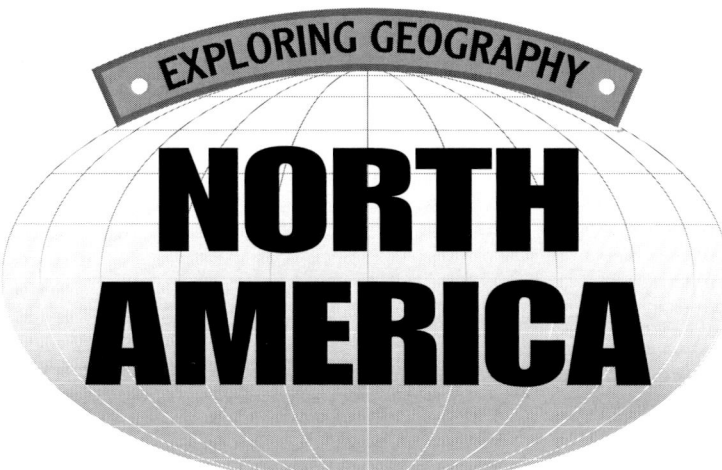

EXPLORING GEOGRAPHY
NORTH AMERICA

CONTENTS

What's in this book 4

Section 1: North America in the world 5–16

Section 2: Political divisions of North America 17–42

Section 3: Physical features of North America 43–68

Section 4: Valuable resources of North America 69–90

Section 5: North American culture 91–110

Section 6: Assessment 111–114

Section 7: Note-takers 115–120

Answers 121–126

CURRICULUM LINKS

COUNTRY	SUBJECT	LEVEL	OBJECTIVES
England	Geography	KS 2	• locate the world's countries, using maps to focus on Europe and North and South America, concentrating on their environmental regions, key physical and human characteristics, countries and major cities
			• identify the position and significance of latitude, longitude, Equator, Northern Hemisphere, Southern Hemisphere, the Tropics of Cancer and Capricorn, Arctic and Antarctic Circle, and the Prime/Greenwich Meridian
			• understand geographical similarities and differences through the study of human and physical geography in a region of the United Kingdom, a region in a European country, and a region within North or South America
			• describe and understand key aspects of physical geography, including: climate zones, biomes and vegetation belts, rivers, mountains, volcanoes and earthquakes
			• describe and understand key aspects of human geography, including: types of settlement and land use, economic activity and the distribution of natural resources
			• use maps, atlases and globes to locate countries and describe features studied
			• use the eight points of a compass and symbols and key to build knowledge of the United Kingdom and the wider world

Prim-Ed Publishing   www.prim-ed.com   Exploring geography: North America   **1**

CURRICULUM LINKS

COUNTRY	SUBJECT	LEVEL	OBJECTIVES
Northern Ireland	The World Around Us	KS 1	• explore the interdependence of people and the environment • explore the effect of people on the natural environment over time • explore how place influences plant and animal life • explore features of the immediate world and comparisons between places • explore sources of energy in the world • study the life of a child in a contrasting location, including similarities and differences such as events and celebrations • compare the local area and a contrasting place; e.g. weather, landscape features
		KS 2	• explore the interdependence of people and the environment • explore the effect of people on the natural environment over time • explore how place influences the nature of life • explore features of, and variations in places, including physical, human, climatic, vegetation and animal life • know how we are interdependent with other parts of Europe and the wider world for some of our goods • compare places, such as location, size and resources • study weather in the local area compared to places that experience very different weather conditions • examine the effect of extreme weather conditions in the wider world, including the effect on places
Republic of Ireland	Geography	3rd/4th Class	• develop some awareness of the human and natural features of some places in other places in the world • establish and use cardinal compass points • develop familiarity with, and engage in practical use of maps • develop an understanding of and use some common map features and conventions • identify major geographical features and find places on the globe • develop some awareness of weather and climate in other parts of the world • develop some awareness of the types of environment which exist in other parts of the world
		5th/6th Class	• become familiar with the natural and human features of some places in other parts of the world • acquire an understanding of the relative location and size of major natural and human features • begin to develop an understanding of the names and relative location of some natural and human features of the world • develop some awareness of directions in wider environments • develop familiarity with, and engage in practical use of, maps • develop an understanding of and use common map features and conventions • recognise key lines of latitude and longitude on the globe • study some aspects of the environments and lives of people in one location in another part of the world • become familiar with the names and approximate location of a small number of major world physical features • become aware of the characteristics of some major climatic regions in different parts of the world

CURRICULUM LINKS

COUNTRY	SUBJECT	LEVEL	OBJECTIVES
Scotland	Social Studies	First	• explore climate zones around the world, and describe how climate affects living things • explore a natural environment different from their own, and discover how the physical features influence the variety of living things
		Second	• study a contrasting area outwith Britain and investigate the main features of weather and climate, discussing the impact on living things • interpret information from different maps, and locate key features within the UK, Europe or wider world
Wales	Geography	KS 2	• identify and locate places and environments using globes, atlases and maps • identify and describe natural and human features • identify similarities and differences to describe, compare and contrast places and environments • study living in other countries – contrasting localities outside the United Kingdom

NOTES

What's in this book

▶ **5 sections** of reproducible information and activity pages centred on five main topics: North America in the world, Political divisions, Physical features, Valuable resources and Culture.

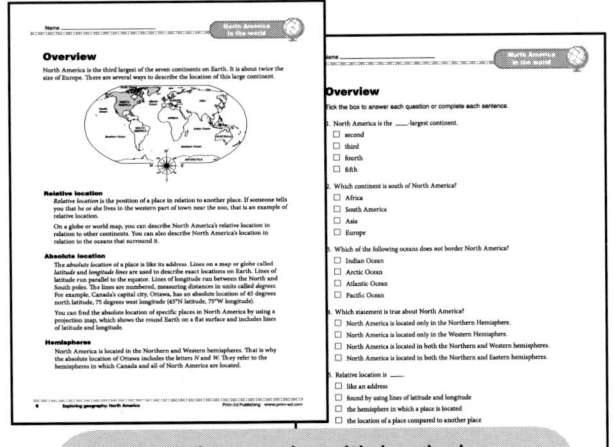

An overview and multiple-choice activity introduces each section.

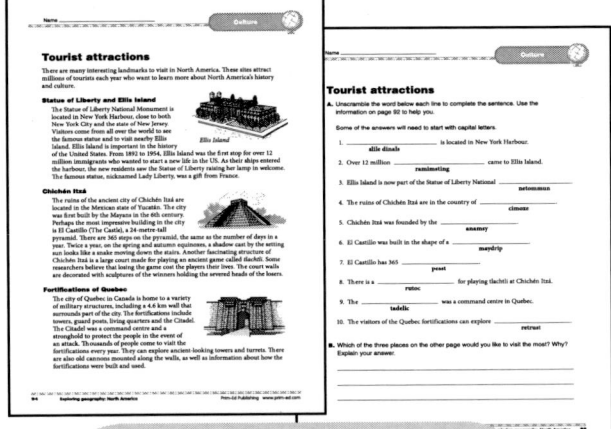

A variety of information and activity pages help pupils explore specific topics in depth.

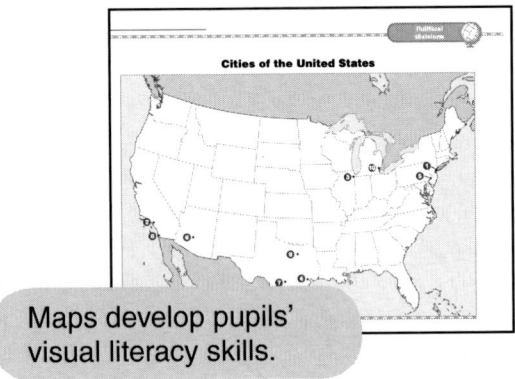

Maps develop pupils' visual literacy skills.

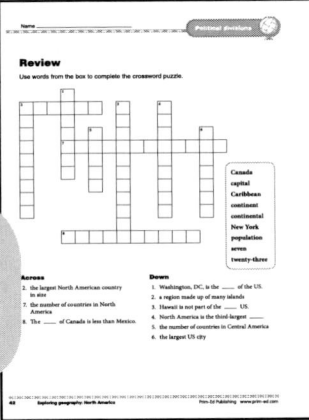

A crossword puzzle at the end of each section provides a fun review activity.

▶ **1 section** of assessment activities

▶ **1 section** of open-ended note-takers

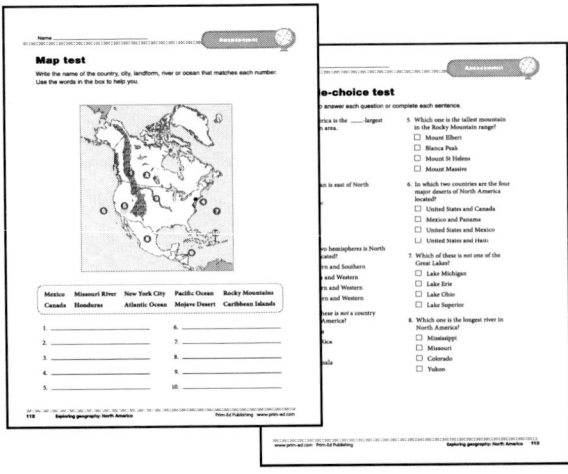

A map quiz and multiple-choice test help assess pupil knowledge.

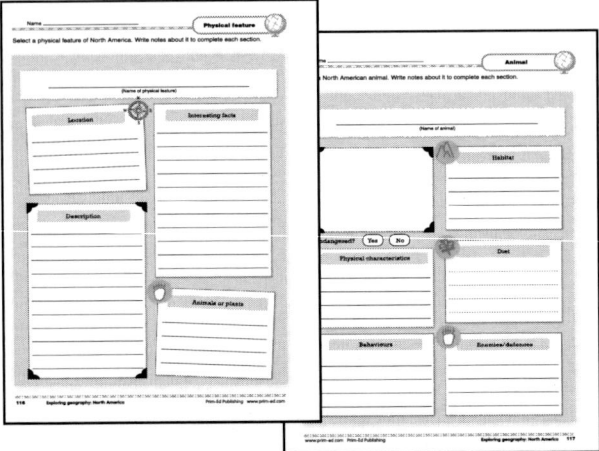

Note-takers allow pupils to research and extend their study.

www.prim-ed.com Prim-Ed Publishing   Exploring geography: **North America** 4

North America in the world

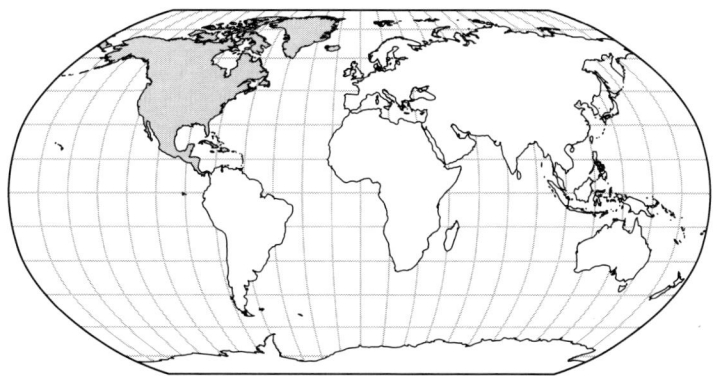

This section introduces pupils to the location of North America in the world. Pupils learn about the difference between relative and absolute location, as well as the hemispheres in which North America lies. Pupils also practise using lines of latitude and longitude to find places on a map.

CONTENTS

Overview 6–7
North America's relative location 8–9
North America's hemispheres . 10–11
North America's absolute location 12–13
Using a projection map 14–15
Review 16

Name _____

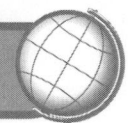

North America in the world

Overview

North America is the third largest of the seven continents on Earth. It is about twice the size of Europe. There are several ways to describe the location of this large continent.

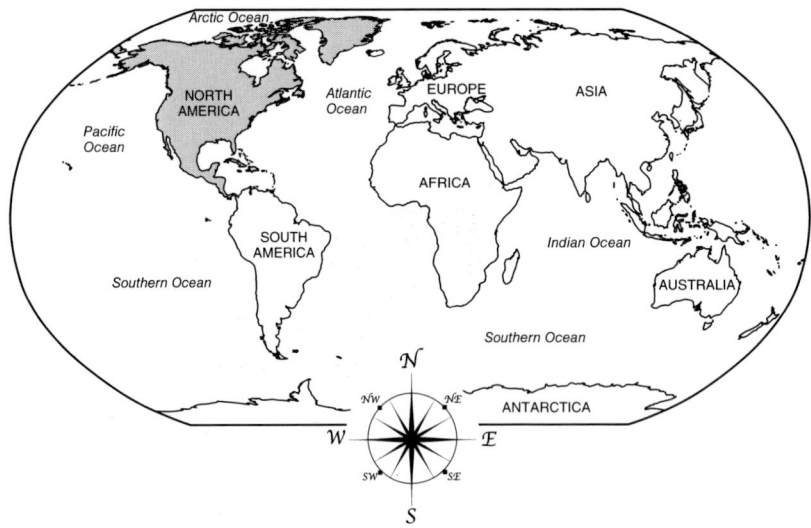

Relative location

Relative location is the position of a place in relation to another place. If someone tells you that he or she lives in the western part of town near the zoo, that is an example of relative location.

On a globe or world map, you can describe North America's relative location in relation to other continents. You can also describe North America's location in relation to the oceans that surround it.

Absolute location

The *absolute location* of a place is like its address. Lines on a map or globe called *latitude* and *longitude lines* are used to describe exact locations on Earth. Lines of latitude run parallel to the equator. Lines of longitude run between the North and South poles. The lines are numbered, measuring distances in units called *degrees*. For example, Canada's capital city, Ottawa, has an absolute location of 45 degrees north latitude, 75 degrees west longitude (45°N latitude, 75°W longitude).

You can find the absolute location of specific places in North America by using a projection map, which shows the round Earth on a flat surface and includes lines of latitude and longitude.

Hemispheres

North America is located in the Northern and Western hemispheres. That is why the absolute location of Ottawa includes the letters *N* and *W*. They refer to the hemispheres in which Canada and all of North America are located.

Name _____

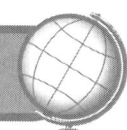

North America in the world

Overview

Tick the box to answer each question or complete each sentence.

1. North America is the _____-largest continent.
   ☐ second
   ☐ third
   ☐ fourth
   ☐ fifth

2. Which continent is south of North America?
   ☐ Africa
   ☐ South America
   ☐ Asia
   ☐ Europe

3. Which of the following oceans does *not* border North America?
   ☐ Indian Ocean
   ☐ Arctic Ocean
   ☐ Atlantic Ocean
   ☐ Pacific Ocean

4. Which statement is true about North America?
   ☐ North America is located only in the Northern Hemisphere.
   ☐ North America is located only in the Western Hemisphere.
   ☐ North America is located in both the Northern and Western hemispheres.
   ☐ North America is located in both the Northern and Eastern hemispheres.

5. Relative location is _____.
   ☐ like an address
   ☐ found by using lines of latitude and longitude
   ☐ the hemisphere in which a place is located
   ☐ the location of a place compared to another place

www.prim-ed.com Prim-Ed Publishing   Exploring geography: North America   **7**

Name _____

North America in the world

North America's relative location

Relative location is the position of a place in relation to another place. How would you describe where North America is located in the world using relative location?

Look at the world map on page 9. One way to describe North America's relative location is to name the other continents that border it. For example, North America is west of Europe and north of South America.

Another way to describe the relative location of North America is to name the oceans that surround the continent. For example, the Atlantic Ocean is east of North America, and the Pacific Ocean is west of it.

A. Use the map on page 9 to complete this paragraph about the relative location of North America.

North America is the third-largest continent in the world. It is located directly west of the continent of _____. South America is to the _____ of North America. To the north is the cold _____ Ocean, while the Atlantic Ocean is _____ of North America. The _____ Ocean borders the continent to the west.

B. Follow the directions to colour the map on the other page.

1. Colour the continent south of North America orange.
2. Use blue to circle the name of the ocean that is east of North America.
3. Draw a lion on the continent that is across the ocean from and south-east of North America.
4. A narrow strip of land connects North America to South America. Circle it with yellow.
5. Greenland is a large North American island to the north-east of the main part of the continent. Colour Greenland green.

8 Exploring geography: North America Prim-Ed Publishing www.prim-ed.com

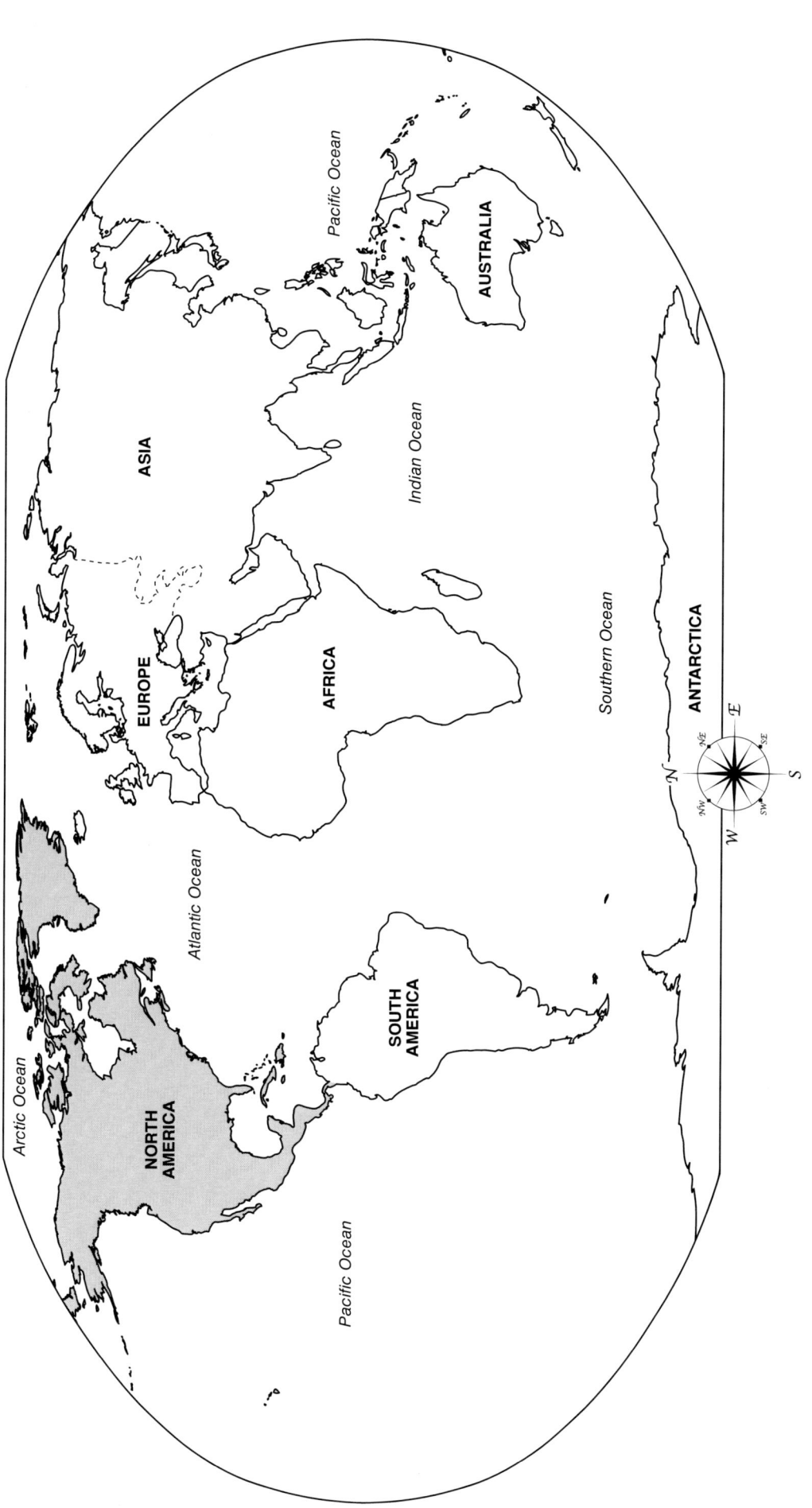

Name _____

North America in the world

North America's hemispheres

On a globe, the Earth is divided into four hemispheres by a horizontal line called the *equator* and by vertical lines that run from the North Pole to the South Pole. The hemispheres are the Northern, Southern, Western and Eastern. North America is in the Northern Hemisphere because it is north of the equator. North America is also located in the Western Hemisphere.

Northern and Southern hemispheres

A globe shows an imaginary horizontal line that runs around the centre of the Earth. This line is called the equator. The equator divides Earth into the Northern and Southern hemispheres.

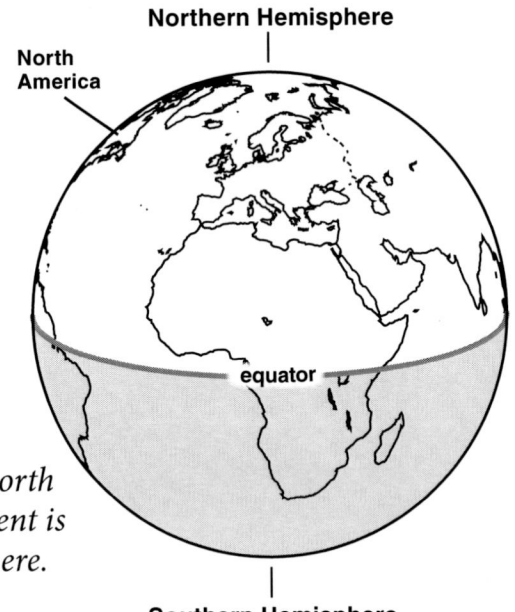

Since North America is north of the equator, the continent is in the Northern Hemisphere.

Western and Eastern hemispheres

A globe also shows imaginary vertical lines that run from the North Pole, the northernmost point on Earth, to the South Pole. One of these lines is called the *prime meridian*. This line, along with its twin line on the opposite side of the globe, creates the Western and Eastern hemispheres.

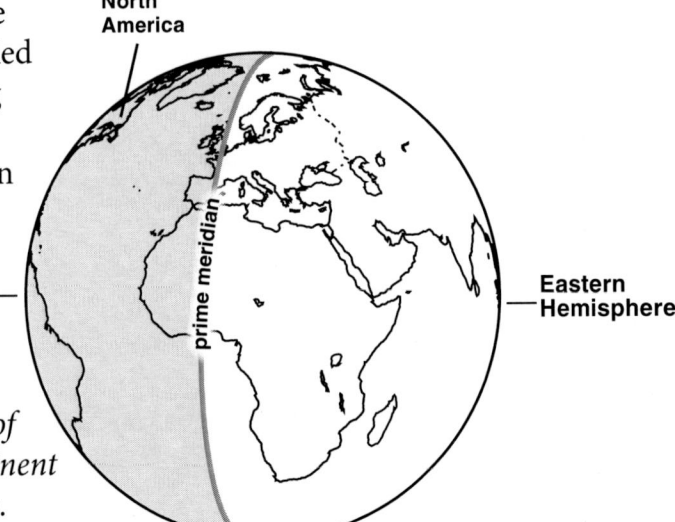

Since North America is west of the prime meridian, the continent is in the Western Hemisphere.

10   Exploring geography: North America   Prim-Ed Publishing   www.prim-ed.com

Name _____

North America in the world

North America's hemispheres

A. Write the letter of the definition that matches each term. Use the information and pictures of the globes on page 10 to help you.

____ 1. North America
____ 2. continent
____ 3. globe
____ 4. equator
____ 5. Western Hemisphere
____ 6. hemisphere
____ 7. North Pole
____ 8. Northern Hemisphere
____ 9. prime meridian

(a) an imaginary line that runs from the North Pole to the South Pole
(b) half of the Earth
(c) the continent that is in both the Northern and Western hemispheres
(d) the hemisphere that is west of the prime meridian
(e) an imaginary line that divides Earth into the Northern and Southern hemispheres
(f) one of the seven large landmasses of Earth
(g) the northernmost point on Earth
(h) a round model of the Earth
(i) the hemisphere that is north of the equator

B. Label the parts of the globe. Use the letters next to the terms in the box.

A. Western Hemisphere
B. North America
C. Northern Hemisphere
D. equator
E. prime meridian

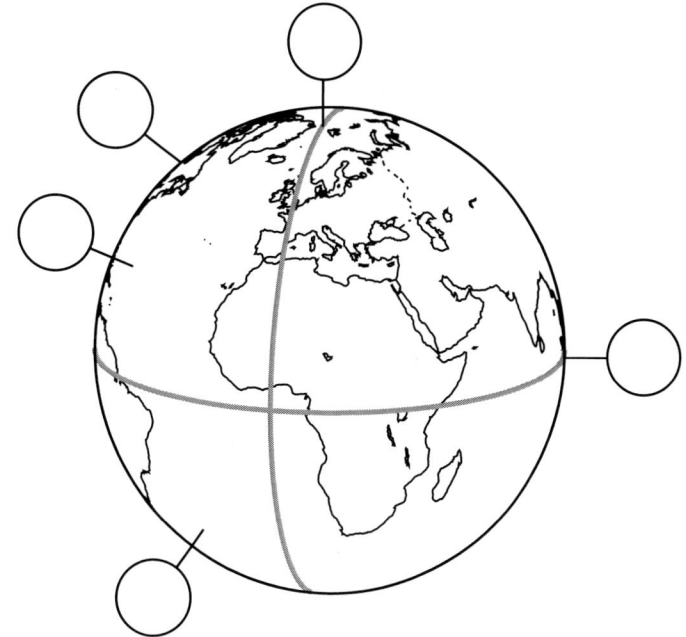

www.prim-ed.com   Prim-Ed Publishing   Exploring geography: North America   11

Name _____

North America in the world

North America's absolute location

Many globes contain lines that make it easier to find specific places on Earth. Lines of latitude measure the distance north and south of the equator. Lines of longitude measure the distance west and east of the prime meridian. You can use lines of latitude and longitude to find the absolute location of North America on a globe.

Latitude

The equator is found at the absolute location of 0° (zero degrees) latitude. Other lines of latitude run parallel to the equator and are labelled with an *N* or *S*, depending on whether they are north or south of the equator. Latitude lines are also called *parallels*.

On the picture of the globe, notice the lines of latitude. Look for the continent of North America. Since the entire continent is north of the equator, all the latitude lines used to find North America's absolute location are labelled in *degrees north*, or °N.

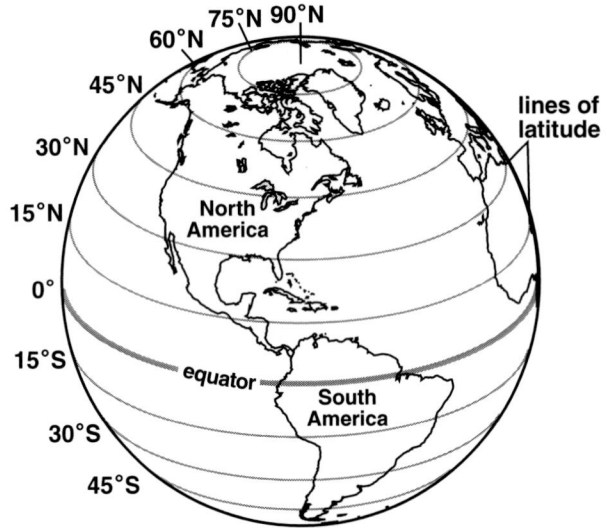

Lines of latitude (parallels)

Longitude

The prime meridian runs from the North Pole to the South Pole at 0° (zero degrees) longitude. Other lines of longitude run north and south, too, and are labelled with an *E* or *W*, depending on whether they are east or west of the prime meridian. Longitude lines are also called *meridians*.

On the picture of the globe, notice the lines of longitude. Look for the continent of North America. Since the entire continent is west of the prime meridian, all of the longitude lines used to find North America's absolute location are labelled in *degrees west*, or °W.

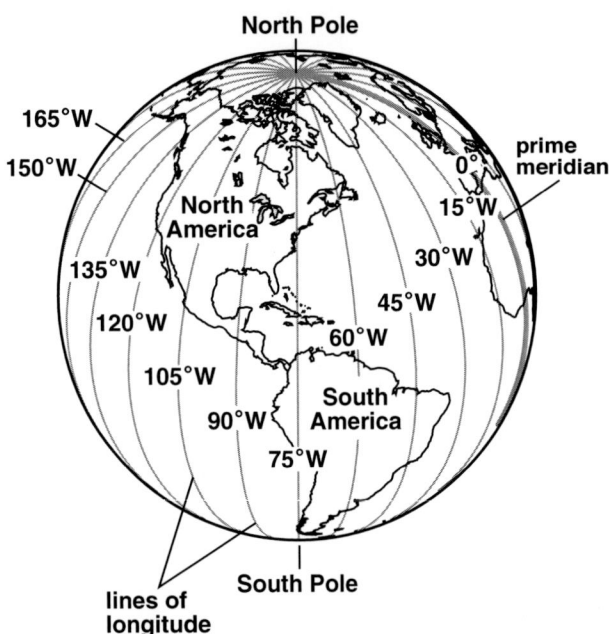

Lines of longitude (meridians)

12   Exploring geography: North America   Prim-Ed Publishing   www.prim-ed.com

Name _____

North America in the world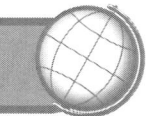

North America's absolute location

To find the absolute location of a place, read the latitude line first and then read the longitude line. For example, the latitude 25°N runs through the southern part of the United States of America. The longitude 80°W runs through the eastern part of the USA. So the absolute location of the south-eastern USA, or the state of Florida, is 25°N latitude, 80°W longitude.

A. Circle the answer to each question. Use the pictures of the globes and information on page 12 to help you.

1. Which line is at zero degrees latitude?	equator	prime meridian
2. Which line runs north and south?	equator	prime meridian
3. Which line of longitude runs through North America?	100°E	100°W
4. Where is the North Pole located?	90°S	90°N
5. Which lines run parallel to the equator?	latitude lines	longitude lines
6. How many degrees are between each line of latitude and longitude on the globes?	10 degrees	15 degrees
7. What is another name for *lines of latitude*?	meridians	parallels
8. Which line of latitude is closer to the equator?	40°N	60°S
9. Which line of longitude is further west?	150°W	120°W

B. Using the information on page 12, explain why all places in North America have absolute locations that are labelled in degrees north and west.

_____

_____

www.prim-ed.com   Prim-Ed Publishing   Exploring geography: North America   13

Name _____

North America in the world

Using a projection map

How do you draw a picture of a round object, like Earth, on a flat piece of paper? In order to show all of Earth's continents and oceans in one view, map makers use a system called *projection*. Mapping the round Earth on a flat surface causes some areas to look bigger than they really are. For example, land near the poles gets stretched out when flattened. That's why Greenland and Antarctica look so big on some maps.

A projection map of the world shows all the lines of latitude and longitude on Earth. Study the projection map on the other page. Notice the lines of latitude and longitude. You can use these lines to find the absolute location of a specific place in North America. For example; the label *North America* is located at 45°N latitude, 105°W longitude.

Read each statement. Circle **yes** if it is true or **no** if it is false. Use the map on page 15 to help you.

1. North America is located on the prime meridian.   **Yes   No**

2. North America is located north of the equator.   **Yes   No**

3. All of the southern part of North America is between the latitudes of 15°S and 30°S.   **Yes   No**

4. North America is the only continent west of the prime meridian.   **Yes   No**

5. North America shares some of the same north latitude lines with Asia.   **Yes   No**

6. North America shares some of the same west longitude lines with Europe.   **Yes   No**

7. The longitude line 60°E runs through North America and South America.   **Yes   No**

8. The latitude line 45°N runs through North America, Europe, and Asia.   **Yes   No**

9. The latitude line 75°N runs through North America and the Arctic Ocean.   **Yes   No**

10. The latitude line 60°S does not run through any continent.   **Yes   No**

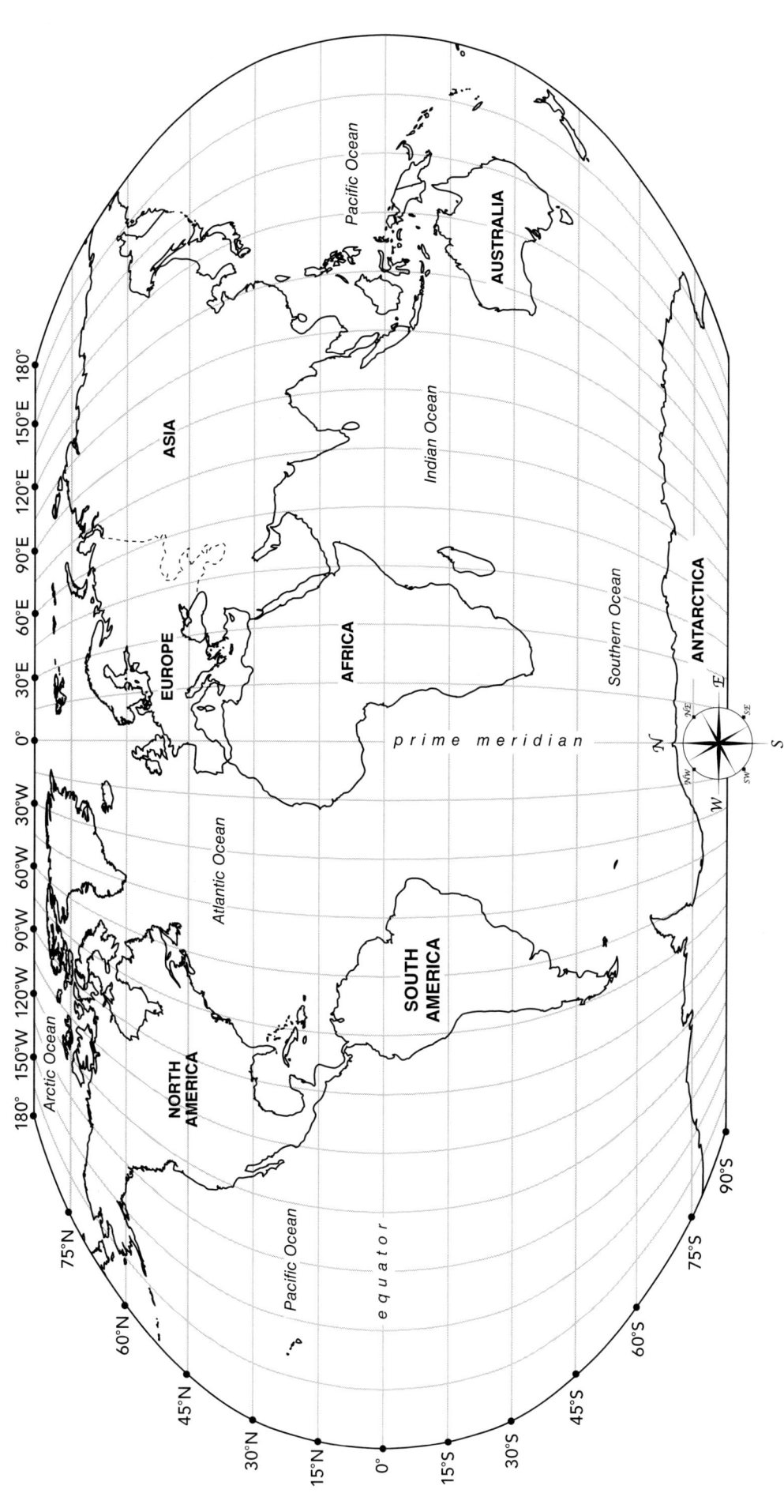

Name _____

North America in the world

Review

Use words from the box to complete the crossword puzzle.

Word box:
Atlantic
equator
Europe
hemisphere
Pacific
projection
relative
third

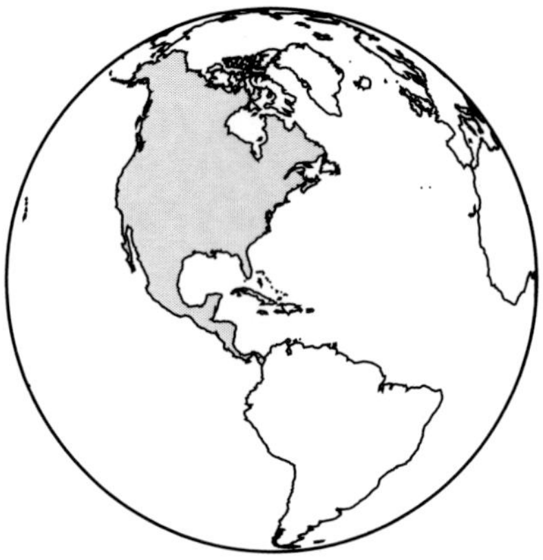

Across

2. A ____ map shows the round Earth on a flat surface.

3. The Arctic, Atlantic and ____ oceans border North America.

5. North America is located in the Northern ____.

7. North America is the ____-largest continent in the world.

8. If you go east of North America, you will find the continent of ____.

Down

1. The ____ Ocean is east of North America.

4. The ____ location is a description of a place using the relation of one place to another.

6. The ____ is the imaginary line that divides the Northern and Southern hemispheres.

16 Exploring geography: North America   Prim-Ed Publishing www.prim-ed.com

Political divisions of North America

This section introduces pupils to the five regions and 23 countries of North America. Pupils learn how each region is unique and study information about the largest countries in size and population. Pupils also learn that the population of North America varies significantly by region.

CONTENTS

Overview 18–19	Cities of the United States of America 32–33
Population of North America 20–21	Mexico 34–35
Countries of North America 22–23	Central America 36–37
Largest countries by area 24–25	The Caribbean 38–39
Largest countries by population 26–27	Capital cities of North America 40–41
Canada and Greenland 28–29	Review 42
The United States of America and its territories 30–31	

Name _____

Political divisions

Overview

North America is the third-largest continent in size and the fourth-largest in population.

- North America covers about 16% of the world's landmass.
- North America has about 8% of the world's people—530 million.

The five regions

The 23 countries in North America can be divided into five regions.

Region	Number of Countries
Canada and Greenland	1 country (Greenland is a territory of Denmark)
United States of America	1 country
Mexico	1 country
Central America	7 countries
Caribbean	13 countries and many small island territories

Where people live

Over half the people who live in North America live in the United States of America. The eastern half of the USA is more densely populated than the west, especially near the northern Atlantic coast and the Great Lakes. The largest city in the United States is New York City, which is part of New York State. There are more than 8 million people in New York City.

Mexico also has a large population, with most people living in urban areas. Mexico City is the country's largest city, with a population of over 8 million people. Very few people live in Greenland and in the colder areas of Canada.

Name _____

Political divisions

Overview

Tick the box to complete each sentence.

1. North America is the ____-largest continent in size.
   - ☐ second
   - ☐ third
   - ☐ fourth
   - ☐ fifth

2. There are ____ countries in North America.
   - ☐ 5
   - ☐ 13
   - ☐ 23
   - ☐ 50

3. Over half the people in North America live in ____.
   - ☐ the United States of America
   - ☐ Canada
   - ☐ Mexico
   - ☐ Central America

4. Most people in Mexico live ____.
   - ☐ in the country
   - ☐ in urban areas
   - ☐ by the beach
   - ☐ in Mexico City

5. The two largest cities in North America are ____.
   - ☐ New York and Los Angeles
   - ☐ New York and Toronto
   - ☐ Mexico City and Los Angeles
   - ☐ Mexico City and New York

Name _____

Political divisions

Population of North America

Between 1950 and 2010, the world population nearly tripled to almost 7 billion. That number is expected to increase to 9 billion by 2050. While the population of North America is also growing, the rate of growth is slower than that of the world. In 1950, there were about 220 million people living in North America. The population is expected to be about 742 million by 2050.

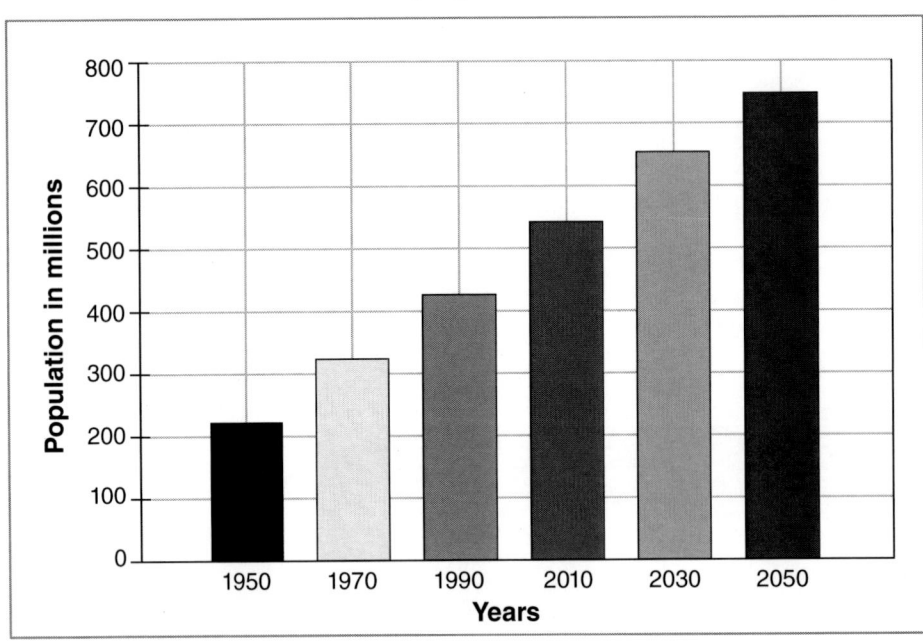

US Bureau of the Census, International Data Base

A. Write two questions that can be answered by using the information on the graph. Then write the answers.

1. _____

2. _____

20   Exploring geography: North America   Prim-Ed Publishing   www.prim-ed.com

Name _____

Political divisions

Population of North America

B. Circle the answer that completes each sentence. Use the information on page 20 to help you.

1. The population of the world has nearly ____ since 1950.

    doubled   **tripled**   **quadrupled**

2. It is predicted that there will be about 9 billion people in the world by ____.

    2030   **2050**   **2070**

3. The population of North America is growing at a ____ rate.

    steady   **rapid**   **record-breaking**

4. In 1950, there were about ____ million people living in North America.

    321   **458**   **220**

5. In 2010, there were over ____ million people in North America.

    500   **600**   **700**

6. By 2030, there will be about ____ million people in North America.

    423   **649**   **742**

7. There are about ____ times as many people living in North America now as there were in 1950.

    two   **three**   **four**

8. There will be about 742 million people living in North America by ____.

    2030   **2050**   **1960**

www.prim-ed.com   Prim-Ed Publishing   Exploring geography: North America   21

Name _____

Political divisions

Countries of North America

North America is made up of 23 countries. Canada is the largest in size, while the smallest is Grenada, a tiny island nation in the Caribbean Sea. The United States of America is the second-largest country in size and includes a main landmass, known as the continental United States, as well as Alaska, Hawaii, Puerto Rico and the US Virgin Islands. Greenland is another part of North America, but it is not a country. It is an independent territory of the Kingdom of Denmark, which is located in Europe.

Region	Countries
Canada and Greenland	Canada
Caribbean	Antigua and Barbuda* Bahamas Barbados Cuba Dominica Dominican Republic Grenada Haiti Jamaica Saint Kitts and Nevis* Saint Lucia Saint Vincent and the Grenadines* Trinidad and Tobago
Central America	Belize Costa Rica El Salvador Guatemala Honduras Nicaragua Panama
Mexico	Mexico
United States	United States of America

* These countries are too small to be labelled on the map.

Find the five regions of North America on the map on page 23. Then use the chart and colour key below to colour the countries.

Colour key

Canada and Greenland: Green   **Mexico:** Red
Central America: Orange   **United States:** Blue
Caribbean: Yellow

Name _____

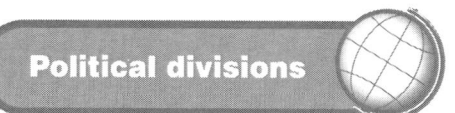

Countries of North America

Name _____

Political divisions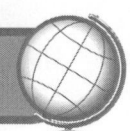

Largest countries by area

North America has some of the world's largest countries in terms of square kilometres. In fact, two of the four largest countries in the world—Canada and the United States—are in North America.

Rank in size	Country	Area in square kilometres
1	Canada	9 984 670
2	United States	9 826 675
3	Mexico	1 964 375
4	Nicaragua	130 370
5	Honduras	112 090

2013 CIA—*The world factbook*

A. Write three statements that can be made by using information in the chart.

1. _____

_____

2. _____

_____

3. _____

_____

B. On the map on page 25, five countries are numbered. The numbers indicate the rank of each country according to size. Colour each country a different colour. Then complete the map key by writing the country names in order from largest to smallest. Include the colour you used for each country.

24   Exploring geography: North America   Prim-Ed Publishing   www.prim-ed.com

Name _____

Political divisions

Largest countries by area

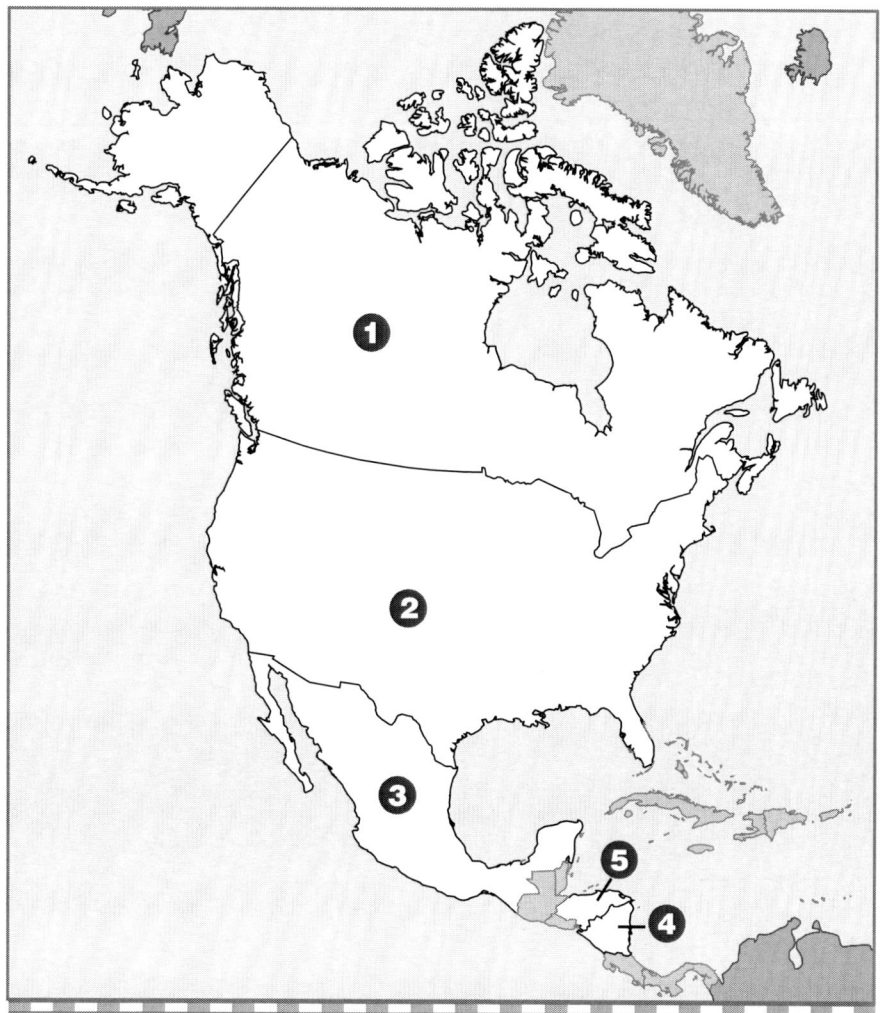

MAP KEY

The five largest countries   Colour

1. _____   _____

2. _____   _____

3. _____   _____

4. _____   _____

5. _____   _____

www.prim-ed.com Prim-Ed Publishing   Exploring geography: North America   25

Name _____

Political divisions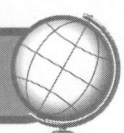

Largest countries by population

The United States is the most populated country in North America. It is also the third most populated country in the world. Mexico is the second most populated country in North America. Although Canada is much bigger in size than Mexico, its population is only about one-third of Mexico's. Of the remaining ten most populated countries in North America, four are located in Central America and three are part of the Caribbean.

A. Match each clue to its country and write the letter on the line. Use the information above and the chart on page 27 to help you.

_____ 1. Canada

_____ 2. Cuba

_____ 3. Dominican Republic

_____ 4. El Salvador

_____ 5. Guatemala

_____ 6. Haiti

_____ 7. Honduras

_____ 8. Mexico

_____ 9. Nicaragua

_____ 10. United States

(a) This is the sixth most populated country.

(b) This country has fewer than 6 million people.

(c) This country has over 3 million more people than Cuba.

(d) This country has over 300 million people.

(e) This country has a population of 8 448 465.

(f) This is the third most populated country in North America.

(g) This country has about 11 million people.

(h) This country has a little over 300 000 more people than Nicaragua.

(i) This country has 116 220 947 people.

(j) This country is ranked number 7 in population.

B. Use the chart on page 27 to help you answer the questions.

1. How many countries in North America have populations over 100 million? _____

2. How many countries in North America have populations over 10 million? _____

26 Exploring geography: North America   Prim-Ed Publishing   www.prim-ed.com

Name _____

Political divisions

Largest countries by population

	Country	Population
1	United States	316 668 567
2	Mexico	116 220 947
3	Canada	34 568 211
4	Guatemala	14 373 472
5	Cuba	11 061 886
6	Dominican Republic	10 219 630
7	Haiti	9 893 934
8	Honduras	8 488 465
9	El Salvador	6 108 590
10	Nicaragua	5 788 531

2013 estimates, CIA—*The world factbook*

c. Write three statements about the most populated countries of North America.

1. _____

_____

2. _____

_____

3. _____

_____

www.prim-ed.com   Prim-Ed Publishing   Exploring geography: North America   **27**

Name _____

Political divisions

Canada and Greenland

Although Canada is the second-largest country in the world in terms of area, it is not heavily populated. Approximately 34 million people live in Canada, making it the 37th most populated country in the world. This is because much of Canada is located in the far north where the climate is very cold, making it difficult for people to live there.

Canada is divided into 13 provinces and territories. Some of the more well-known provinces are Alberta, British Columbia, Nova Scotia, Ontario and Quebec. The capital city of Canada is Ottawa. It is located in the province of Ontario.

Although it is located in North America, Greenland belongs to the country of Denmark in Europe. The population of Greenland is only about 57 000.

A. Read each statement. Circle **yes** if it is true or **no** if it is false. Use the information on this page and the map on page 29 to help you.

1. Canada is the 34th most populated country in the world.	Yes	No
2. Canada's capital city is located in the province of Ontario.	Yes	No
3. The province of Alberta has no ocean coastline.	Yes	No
4. Greenland is north-west of Canada.	Yes	No
5. There are 14 provinces and territories in Canada.	Yes	No
6. Alberta, Saskatchewan and Manitoba border the United States.	Yes	No
7. Canada is the largest country in the world.	Yes	No
8. Newfoundland and Labrador is a territory of Denmark.	Yes	No
9. Quebec is larger than Saskatchewan.	Yes	No
10. British Columbia is bordered by the Pacific Ocean.	Yes	No

Name _____

Political divisions

Canada and Greenland

B. Write three facts about Canada and Greenland, using the information on page 28 and this map to help you.

1. _____
   _____

2. _____
   _____

3. _____
   _____

Name _____

Political divisions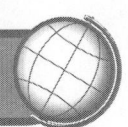

The United States and its territories

The United States of America is a union of 50 states. The continental US is made up of 48 states that occupy the central part of North America. Alaska, located north-west of Canada, and Hawaii, in the mid-Pacific Ocean, are the 49th and 50th states. In addition, the United States possesses five territories. Two of them, Puerto Rico and the US Virgin Islands, are located within the Caribbean region of North America. The other three territories are American Samoa, Guam and the Midway Islands, which are located in the Pacific Ocean.

The 50 states can be grouped into six regions. They are the Pacific (including Alaska and Hawaii), Rocky Mountain, Southwest, North-Central, Southeast and Northeast regions. Washington, DC, the capital of the United States, is located in the Southeast region.

A. Use the information above to complete the paragraph.

The United States is made up of 50 states. The country can be divided into six _____. The _____ of the United States, Washington, DC, is located in the _____ region. The states of _____ and _____ belong to the _____ region and are not a part of the continental US. The United States also has five _____, including Puerto Rico and the _____, which are located in North America.

B. On the map on page 31, colour each of the US regions a different colour. Then colour the key to correctly match the map.

C. Use the map on page 31 to answer the questions.

1. Which region is directly west of North-Central? _____

2. Which region is furthest to the west? _____

3. Which two regions contain the Great Lakes? _____

4. Which two regions border the Atlantic Ocean? _____

30 Exploring geography: North America Prim-Ed Publishing www.prim-ed.com

Political divisions

Name _____

The United States and its territories

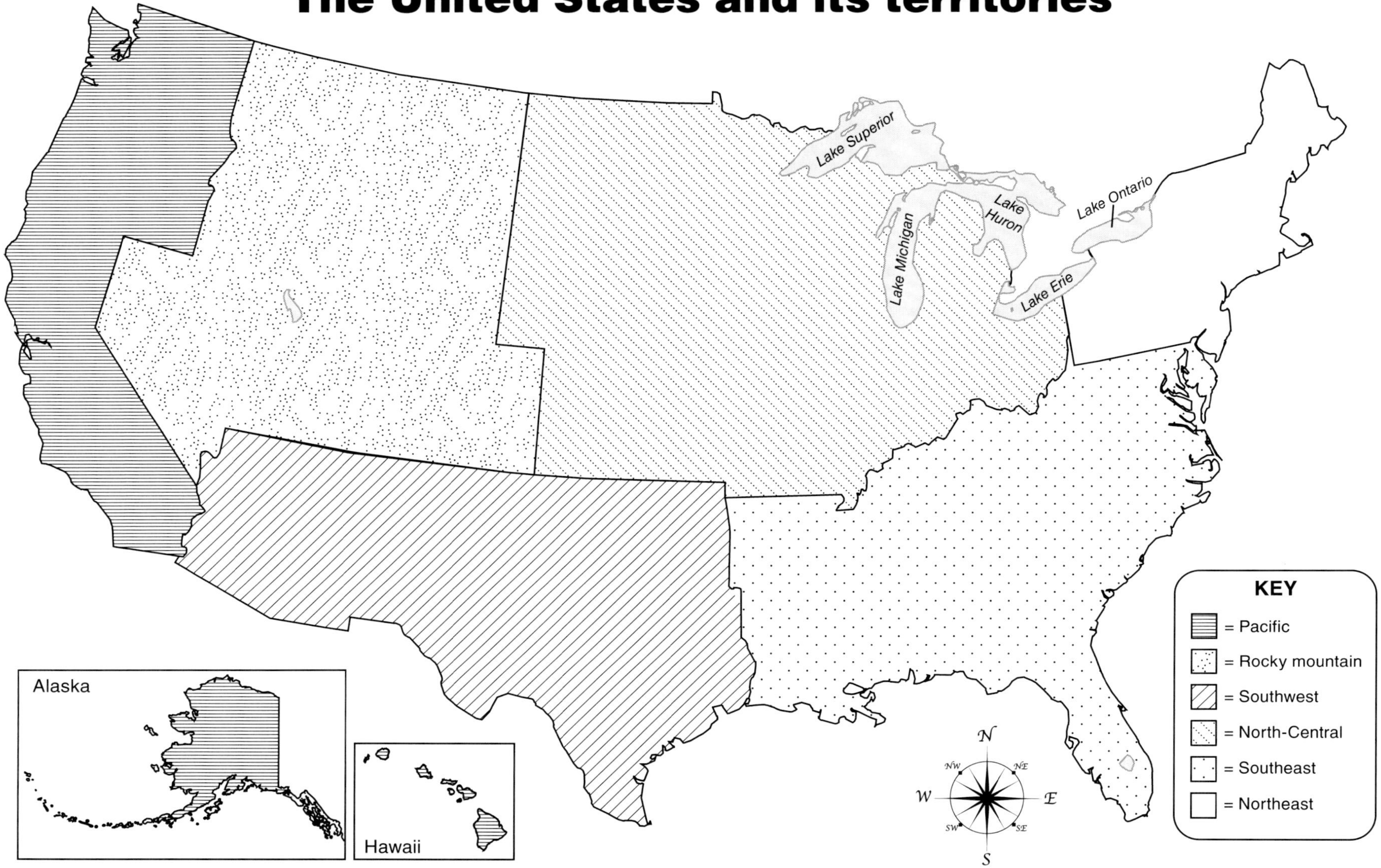

KEY

= Pacific	= Rocky mountain	= Southwest	= North-Central	= Southeast	= Northeast

Lake Ontario
Lake Erie
Lake Huron
Lake Michigan
Lake Superior

Hawaii

Alaska

Prim-Ed Publishing   www.prim-ed.com   Exploring geography: North America   31

Name _____

Political divisions

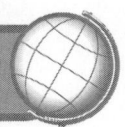

Cities of the United States

Over 300 million people live in the United States. About 80% of these people live in cities or suburbs. More people live in the eastern regions of the country than in other areas. However, more and more people are moving to the west and south. Cities in the Southwest region are starting to become more crowded.

With over 8 million people, New York City is by far the biggest city in the United States. Even Los Angeles, which is the second-biggest city, has fewer than half the number of people of New York. Other heavily populated cities include Chicago, Houston, Philadelphia and Phoenix.

A. Look at the chart showing the populations of the United States' biggest cities. Then write a sentence about the information in the chart.

	City	Population (2011 est.)
1	New York	8 244 910
2	Los Angeles	3 819 702
3	Chicago	2 707 120
4	Houston	2 145 146
5	Philadelphia	1 536 471
6	Phoenix	1 469 471
7	San Antonio	1 359 758
8	San Diego	1 326 179
9	Dallas	1 223 229
10	Detroit	706 585

_____

_____

B. On the map on page 33, a star marks the location of each city, along with its number according to rank in population. Write the name of each city near its star.

Cities of the United States

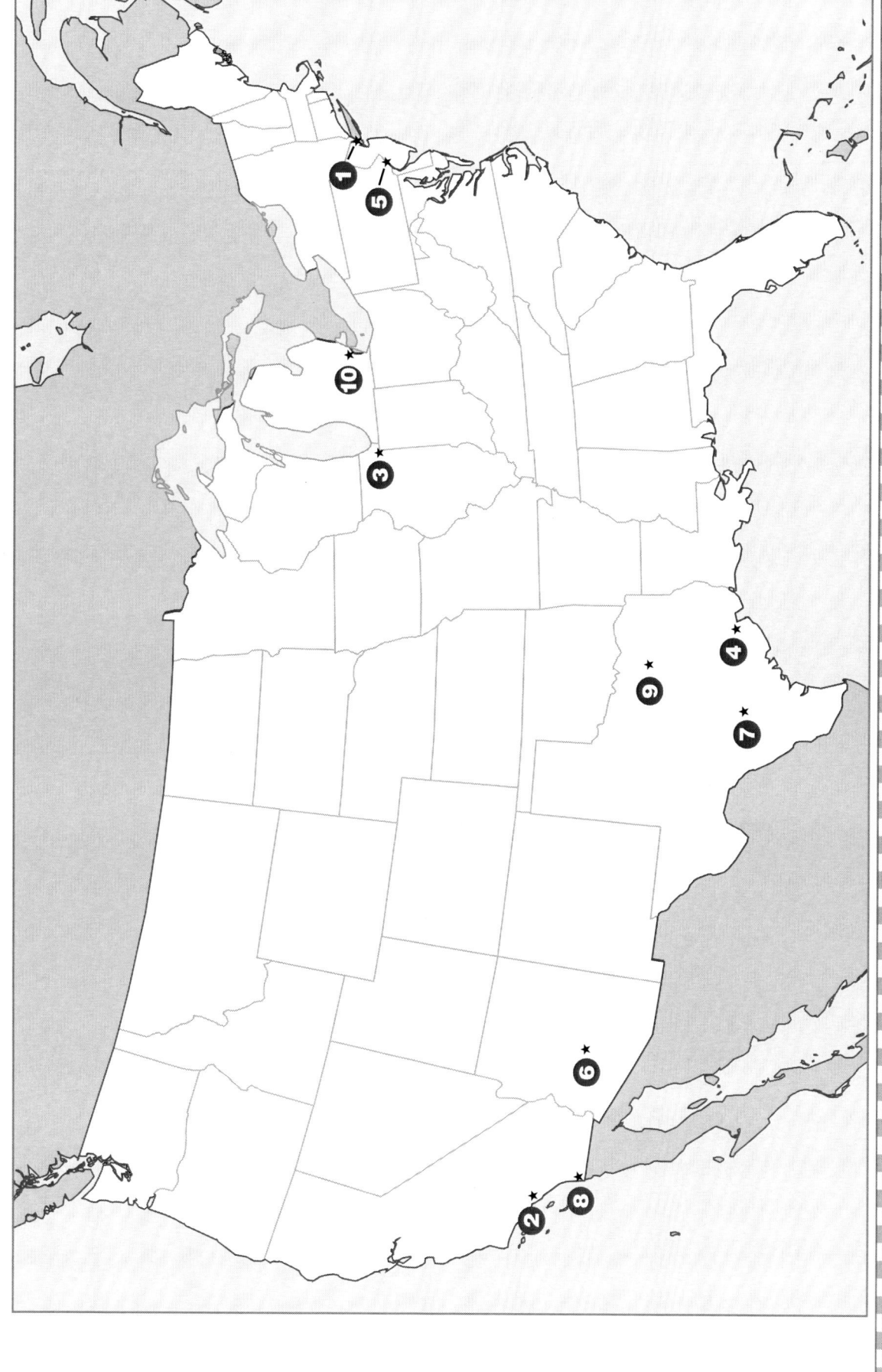

Name _____

Political divisions

Mexico

Mexico is located just south of the United States. In terms of area, Mexico is the third-largest country in North America and the 15th largest in the world. Mexico is made up of 31 states.

Over 116 million people live in Mexico, making it the 11th most populated country in the world. Most people live in the cities. Mexico City, the capital of Mexico, is by far the largest city with more than 8 million people. Other large cities in Mexico include Guadalajara, Monterrey, Puebla, Puerto Vallarta and Tijuana.

A. Use the information above to complete the paragraph.

Mexico is the third-largest country in _____ and the 15th largest in the _____. There are _____ states in Mexico. The capital city of Mexico is _____. It is also the largest city, with more than 8 million people.

B. Circle the answer that completes each sentence. Use the map on page 35 and the information on this page to help you.

1. The state of ___ is bordered by the Pacific Ocean.

   Jalisco   **Hidalgo**

2. The state of Durango is ___ of the state of Oaxaca.

   northwest   **southeast**

3. The state of ___ is at the end of a peninsula.

   Chiapas   **Baja California Sur**

4. ___ is one of the states that borders the United States.

   Veracruz   **Coahuila**

Name _____

Political divisions

Mexico

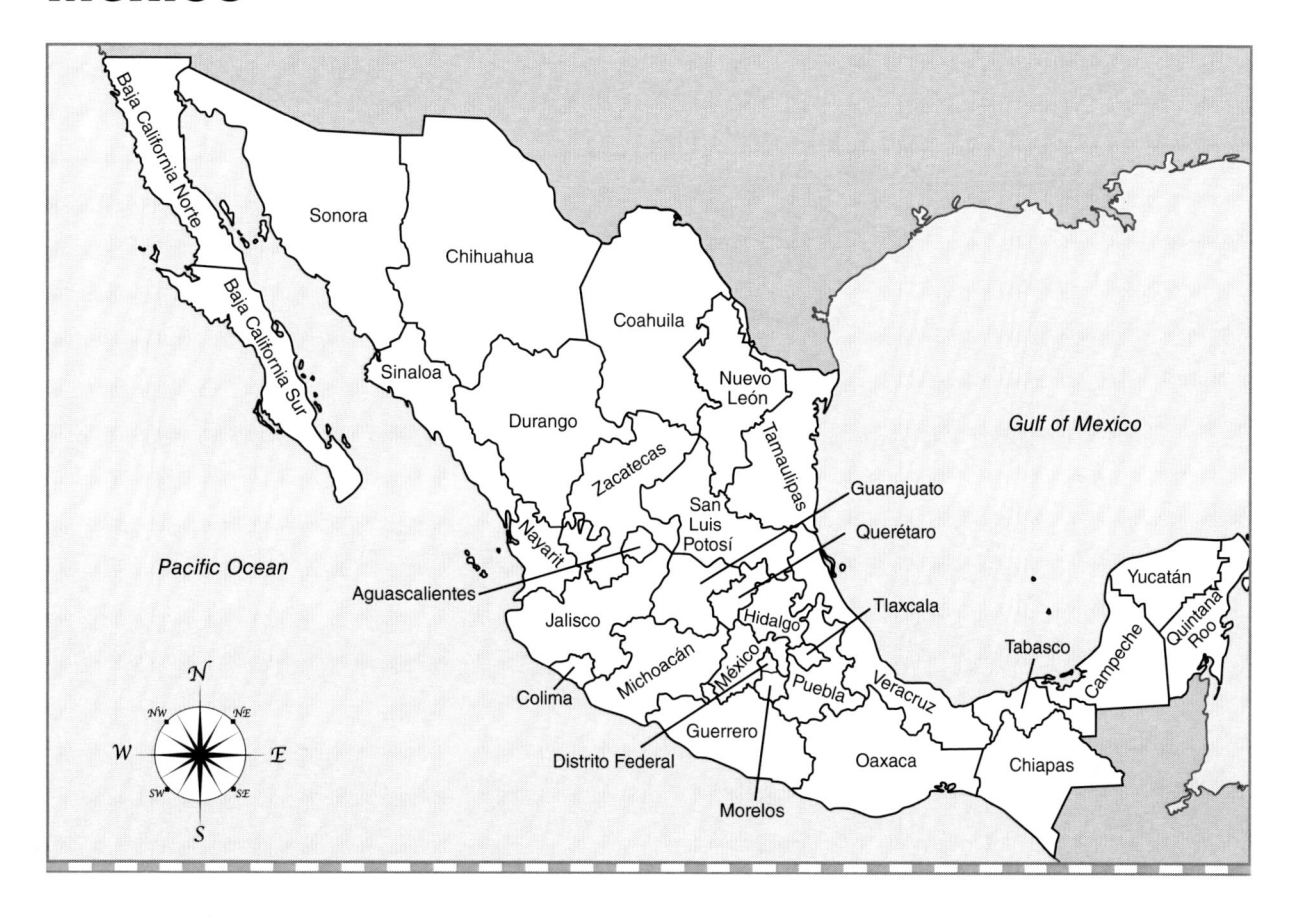

c. The United States borders Mexico to the north. Colour the six Mexican states that border the US. Then write a caption for the map.

_____

_____

_____

www.prim-ed.com Prim-Ed Publishing   Exploring geography: North America **35**

Name _____

Political divisions

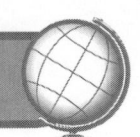

Central America

Central America is a thin band of countries located between Mexico and South America. There are seven countries in Central America. They are Belize, Costa Rica, El Salvador, Guatemala, Honduras, Nicaragua and Panama. Of these, Nicaragua is the largest in area, followed by Honduras and Guatemala.

Guatemala is by far the most populated country in Central America. Over 14 million people live in Guatemala. That is nearly twice the number of people living in the second most populated country, Honduras. With a population of just over 300 000, Belize has the fewest people.

A. Use the chart to rank each country by population and area in order from largest to smallest.

Country	Population	Area in square kilometres
Belize	334 297	22 966
Costa Rica	4 695 942	51 100
El Salvador	6 108 590	21 041
Guatemala	14 373 472	108 889
Honduras	8 448 465	111 864
Nicaragua	5 778 531	130 370
Panama	3 559 408	75 420

2013 est. CIA—*The world factbook*

Population

1. _____
2. _____
3. _____
4. _____
5. _____
6. _____
7. _____

Area

1. _____
2. _____
3. _____
4. _____
5. _____
6. _____
7. _____

Name _____

Political divisions

Central America

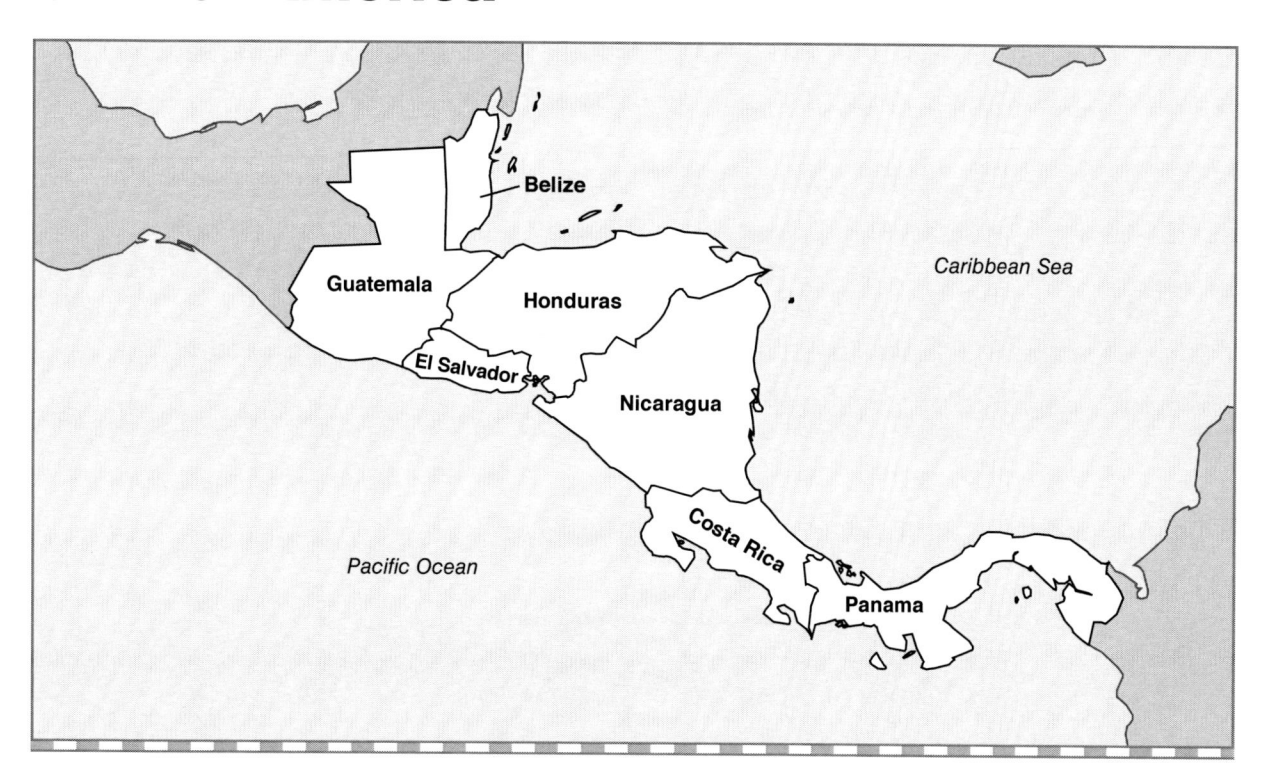

B. Colour each Central American country a different colour. Then write a caption for the map, using the words *area*, *largest* and *smallest*.

_____

_____

_____

C. Use information from the map to help you write two statements about Central America.

1. _____

_____

2. _____

_____

www.prim-ed.com Prim-Ed Publishing   Exploring geography: North America 37

Name _____

Political divisions

The Caribbean

In the Caribbean Sea, east of Central America, there are thousands of islands, many of which are uninhabited. Among these, there are 13 independent nations, as well as 11 territories.

The Caribbean can be divided into three regions: the Bahamas, the Greater Antilles and the Lesser Antilles. The Bahamas is a group of islands south-east of the tip of Florida. The Greater Antilles is west of the Bahamas and includes Cuba, Jamaica, Puerto Rico and Hispaniola, on which both Haiti and the Dominican Republic are located. All of the other Caribbean Islands, including the Virgin Islands, Barbados, and Trinidad and Tobago, are part of the Lesser Antilles.

A. Read each statement. Circle **yes** if it is true or **no** if it is false. Use the information on this page and the map on page 39 to help you.

1.	There are 13 independent nations in the Caribbean.	Yes	No
2.	There are thousands of islands in the Caribbean.	Yes	No
3.	The Bahamas are located south-west of the tip of Florida.	Yes	No
4.	Cuba is part of the Bahamas.	Yes	No
5.	Dominica is an island in the Lesser Antilles.	Yes	No
6.	Haiti and the Dominican Republic are on the island of Hispaniola.	Yes	No
7.	St Lucia is part of the Greater Antilles.	Yes	No
8.	Cuba is south-west of the Bahamas.	Yes	No
9.	Puerto Rico is the furthest east of all the islands.	Yes	No
10.	Guadeloupe is part of the Bahamas.	Yes	No

B. On the map on page 39, colour the islands that make up the Greater Antilles. Then write a caption for the three regions of the Caribbean.

Name _____

Political divisions

The Caribbean

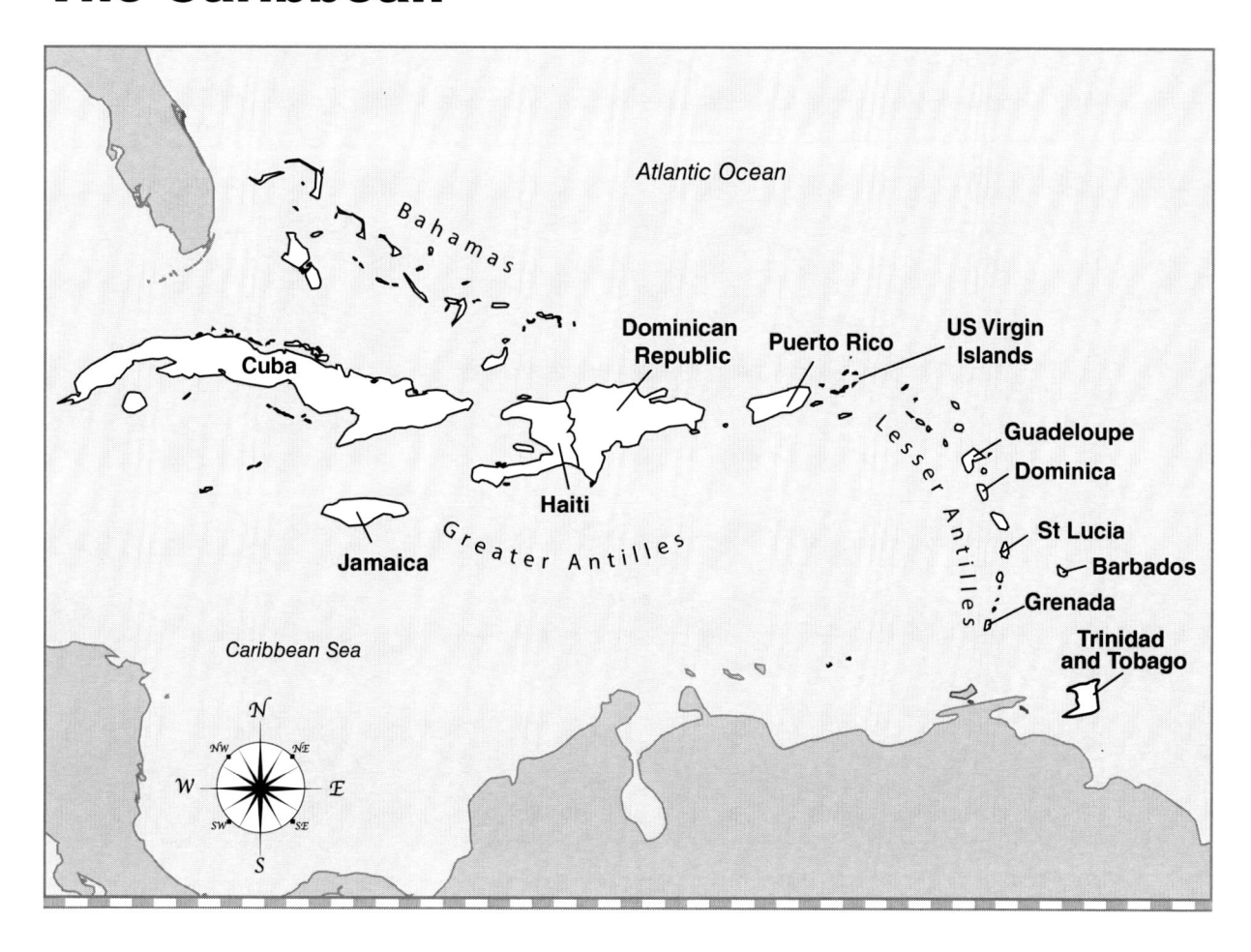

Map showing Caribbean region with labels: Atlantic Ocean, Bahamas, Cuba, Dominican Republic, Puerto Rico, US Virgin Islands, Guadeloupe, Dominica, St Lucia, Barbados, Grenada, Trinidad and Tobago, Haiti, Jamaica, Greater Antilles, Lesser Antilles, Caribbean Sea.

Capital cities of North America

Every country in North America has a capital city, which is the central location of the country's government. The capital city contains government buildings where leaders meet and laws are made. Often the president, prime minister or other leaders of the country live in the capital city.

In many countries, such as Mexico and Cuba, the capital city is also the largest city in the country. However, in other countries, such as Canada and Belize, the capital is *not* the largest city.

North American countries and their capitals

Country	Capital city	Country	Capital city
Antigua and Barbuda	St John's	Haiti	Port-au-Prince
Bahamas	Nassau	Honduras	Tegucigalpa
Barbados	Bridgetown	Jamaica	Kingston
Belize	Belmopan	Mexico	Mexico City
Canada	Ottawa	Nicaragua	Managua
Costa Rica	San José	Panama	Panama City
Cuba	Havana	St Kitts and Nevis	Basseterre
Dominica	Roseau	St Lucia	Castries
Dominican Republic	Santo Domingo	St Vincent and the Grenadines	Kingstown
El Salvador	San Salvador	Trinidad and Tobago	Port-of-Spain
Grenada	St George's	United States	Washington, DC
Guatemala	Guatemala City		

Name _____

Political divisions

Capital cities of North America

A. Use the chart on page 40 to write the capital city that goes with each country.

Costa Rica: _____   United States: _____

Barbados: _____   Mexico: _____

Canada: _____   St Lucia: _____

Belize: _____   Nicaragua: _____

Cuba: _____   Jamaica: _____

Bahamas: _____   Honduras: _____

B. In the word puzzle, find and circle the 12 capital cities you wrote above. Words may appear across, down or diagonally.

```
T E G U C I G A L P A B M
B S O M A N A G U A B R E
E A Q T Z A L Y V K M I X
L N U D T L U S W I H D I
M J G W N A B U A N P G C
O O V M S P W N H G D E O
P S P S C S I A A S L T C
A E A R X C Q N S T M O I
N N M A N A A U M O T W T
W A U O N V V M X N W N Y
P S C A A C A S T R I E S
W A S H I N G T O N D C W
```

www.prim-ed.com Prim-Ed Publishing   Exploring geography: North America 41

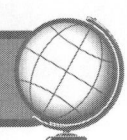

Review

Use words from the box to complete the crossword puzzle.

Word box:
Canada
capital
Caribbean
continent
continental
New York
population
seven
twenty-three

Across

2. the largest North American country in size
7. the number of countries in North America
8. The ___ of Canada is less than Mexico.

Down

1. Washington, DC, is the ___ of the US.
2. a region made up of many islands
3. Hawaii is not part of the ___ US.
4. North America is the third-largest ___.
5. the number of countries in Central America
6. the largest US city

SECTION 3

Physical features of North America

In this section, pupils learn about the landforms and bodies of water of North America. They discover that North America is home to some of the most dramatic landforms on Earth, including the Grand Canyon and the Rocky Mountains. Pupils learn about North America's hot deserts and cold northern tundra and also become familiar with the major lakes and rivers in North America.

CONTENTS

Overview........................44–45	North America's bodies of water..60–61
North America's landscape...........46–47	Great Lakes 62–63
Rocky Mountains........................48–49	North America's rivers 64–65
Grand Canyon 50–51	Panama Canal............................66–67
Deserts of North America.............52–53	Review............................. 68
Frozen north 54–55	
Central America's rainforests........56–57	
Islands of the Caribbean...............58–59	

Name _____

Physical features

Overview

North America is the world's third-largest continent. It is almost completely surrounded by water and is connected to South America by only a thin strip of land. North America has many spectacular natural features.

Landforms

Because of North America's large size, it has a variety of diverse landforms, from island volcanoes to frozen tundra.

North America has several mountain ranges, the longest of which is the Rocky Mountains. Many of the peaks in the Rocky Mountains are over 4267 m tall! However, the tallest mountain in North America is not located in the Rocky Mountains. It is Alaska's Denali, formerly known as Mount McKinley, which is 6194 m tall.

Denali (Mount McKinley)

North America has four major deserts. They are the Chihuahuan, Sonoran, Mojave, and Great Basin. These deserts are located in the south-west United States and Mexico. Three of them are hot deserts, while one, the Great Basin Desert, is a cold desert.

Other landforms include grassy plains in the central United States, huge evergreen forests, which cover much of Canada, and tropical rainforests in Central America. Very little grows in the far northern part of the continent, where the land is frozen tundra.

North America is also home to many islands, including the Caribbean islands in the south-east. Several of these islands have active volcanoes.

Bodies of water

North America is bordered by the Arctic, Pacific and Atlantic oceans. It is also bordered by many seas, including the frigid Bering, Beaufort and Labrador seas to the north, and the warm Caribbean Sea to the south. In addition, there are several large gulfs and bays bordering the continent.

North America is also home to the Great Lakes, which make up the largest system of freshwater lakes in the world. About one-fifth of the world's fresh water supply is in the Great Lakes.

There are also many rivers in North America. At 4023 km long, the Missouri River is the longest river on the continent. Together the Missouri, Mississippi and Ohio rivers make up the third-largest river system in the world.

Name _____

Physical features

Overview

Tick the box to answer each question.

1. Which statement is *not* true?
   - ☐ Denali is over 6000 metres tall.
   - ☐ Denali is in the Rocky Mountains.
   - ☐ Denali is the tallest mountain in North America.
   - ☐ Denali is in Alaska.

2. Which of these is *not* a desert in North America?
   - ☐ Great Basin
   - ☐ Sonoran
   - ☐ Mojave
   - ☐ Sahara

3. Which three oceans border North America?
   - ☐ Pacific, Atlantic, Indian
   - ☐ Pacific, Indian, Arctic
   - ☐ Pacific, Atlantic, Arctic
   - ☐ Atlantic, Arctic, Indian

4. About how much of the world's supply of fresh water is in the Great Lakes?
   - ☐ ¼
   - ☐ ⅕
   - ☐ ⅙
   - ☐ ¹⁄₁₀

5. Which of these is the longest river in North America?
   - ☐ Missouri
   - ☐ Mississippi
   - ☐ Ohio
   - ☐ Denali

Name _____

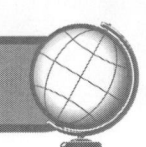

Physical features

North America's landscape

North America has a varied landscape. There are frozen tundras in the far north, where the land is covered in snow and ice for much of the year. There are tall mountains in the west and hot deserts in the south-west. Coniferous forests dominate the northern central area around Hudson Bay. In the midwest of the United States, the land features flat plains.

A. Study the physical map of North America on page 47. Use the map and key to answer the questions.

1. Which mountain range is along the north-western coast of North America? _____

2. Which mountain range is furthest south? _____

3. What is the name of the major mountain peak shown on the map? _____

4. Which landform covers most of the central United States? _____

5. Which island is north of Hudson Bay? _____

6. Which desert is furthest north? _____

7. What is the name of the area that surrounds Hudson Bay? _____

8. Which peninsula is west of the Caribbean Sea? _____

B. Follow the directions to colour the map on page 47.

1. Colour the deserts yellow.

2. Colour the mountains brown.

3. Use light green to circle the plains.

4. Use dark green to circle the Canadian Shield.

Name _____

Physical features

North America's landscape

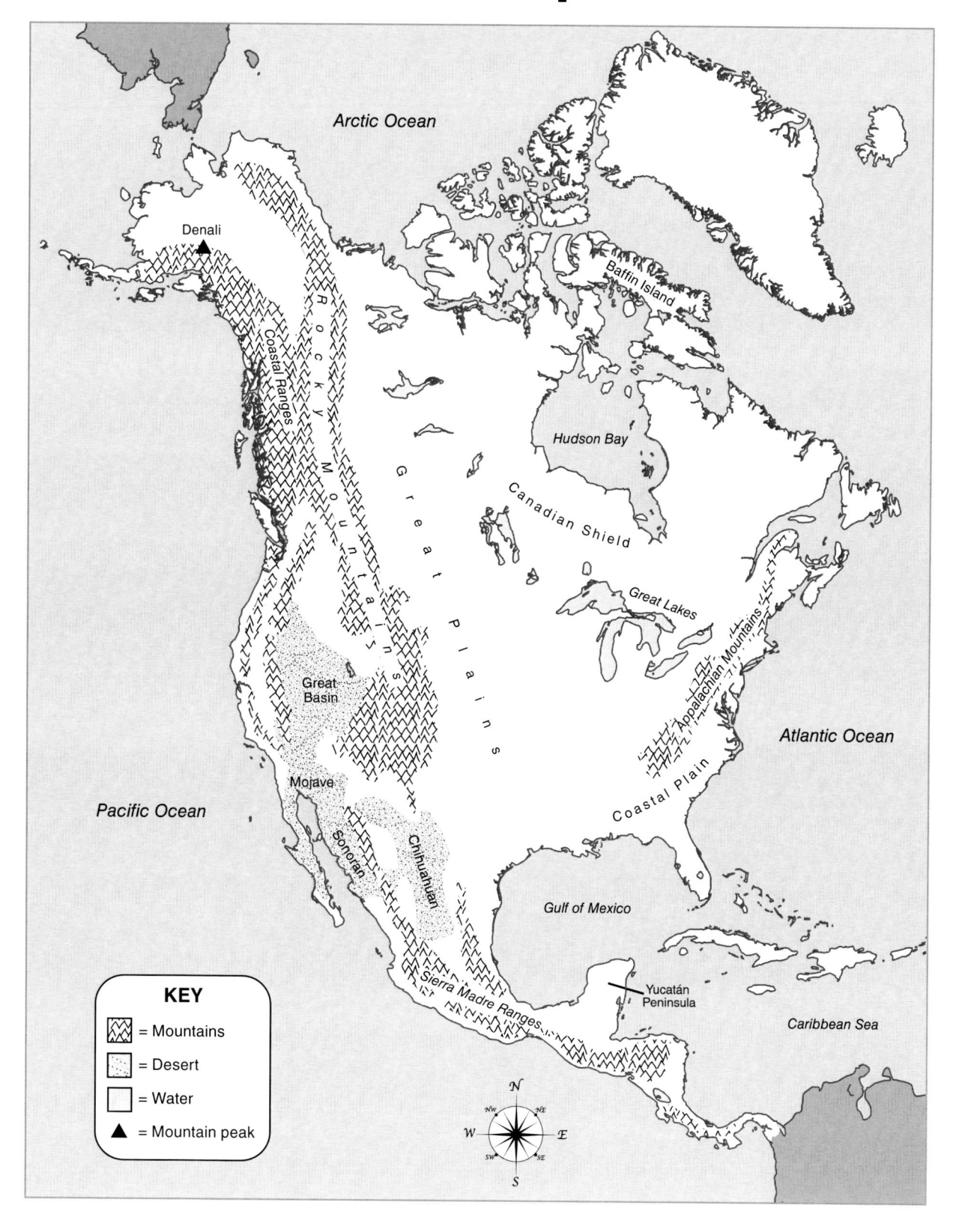

Arctic Ocean

Denali ▲

Baffin Island

Coastal Ranges

Rocky Mountains

Hudson Bay

Canadian Shield

Great Plains

Great Lakes

Appalachian Mountains

Great Basin

Atlantic Ocean

Pacific Ocean

Mojave

Sonoran

Chihuahuan

Coastal Plain

Gulf of Mexico

Sierra Madre Ranges

Yucatán Peninsula

Caribbean Sea

KEY
- ▨ = Mountains
- ⋯ = Desert
- ☐ = Water
- ▲ = Mountain peak

www.prim-ed.com   Prim-Ed Publishing

Exploring geography: North America   47

Rocky Mountains

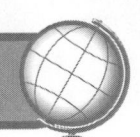

The Rocky Mountains (also called 'the Rockies') form the largest mountain system in North America. They stretch more than 4800 km, from Yukon in northern Canada through the western United States to New Mexico in the south. The Rocky Mountain system is actually made up of over one hundred smaller mountain ranges.

The Rocky Mountains form the Continental Divide. This means that rivers on the west side of the mountains flow west into the Pacific Ocean, while those on the east side flow east into the Atlantic or Arctic oceans.

Many different kinds of animals live on the lower slopes of the Rockies. Only a few animals that can survive in a harsh climate live above the timberline, where trees do not grow. Two of these hardy animals are the Rocky Mountain goat and the bighorn sheep.

At 4402 m, Mount Elbert is the highest of the Rocky Mountains. But Mount Elbert has plenty of company. Twenty-four other mountains are over 4267 m tall. All of these mountains are located in the state of Colorado.

Tallest mountains of the Rockies
(listed in alphabetical order)

Mountain peak	Height in metres
Blanca Peak	4372 m
Crestone Peak	4357 m
Grays Peak	4349 m
La Plata Peak	4377 m
Mt Antero	4349 m
Mt Elbert	4402 m
Mt Harvard	4395 m
Mt Lincoln	4354 m
Mt Massive	4396 m
Uncompahgre Peak	4361 m

Name _____

Physical features

Rocky Mountains

A. Read each statement. Circle **yes** if it is true or **no** if it is false. Use the information on the other page to help you.

1. The Rocky Mountain system is over 4800 km long. Yes   No

2. The Rocky Mountains are in the eastern United States. Yes   No

3. The Continental Divide determines the direction in which rivers flow. Yes   No

4. Mount Massive is the tallest mountain in the Rockies. Yes   No

5. Mount Elbert is over 4500 metres tall. Yes   No

6. Mount Elbert is located in the state of Wyoming. Yes   No

7. Bighorn sheep live above the timberline in the Rocky Mountains. Yes   No

8. Blanca Peak is 4372 metres tall. Yes   No

9. La Plata Peak is taller than Mount Harvard. Yes   No

10. Grays Peak is the same height as Mount Antero. Yes   No

B. Use the chart on page 48 to write the names of the 10 tallest mountains in the Rockies, from largest to smallest.

Rank	Mountain peak
1	
2	
3	
4	
5	

Rank	Mountain peak
6	
7	
8	
9	
10	

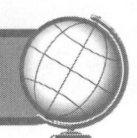

Grand Canyon

The Grand Canyon, located in north-west Arizona, is one of the largest canyons on Earth. It is 446 km long and about 1.6 km deep. The width of the canyon varies. In some spots it is less than 1.6 km wide, while in others it is 29 km across.

The Grand Canyon was formed by a process called erosion. Over millions of years, the Colorado River, which runs through the canyon, wore away at the layers of rock to carve out the canyon. Some of the types of rocks that make up the Grand Canyon include sandstone, shale and limestone. These different rock layers can be clearly seen in the canyon walls. Most are various shades of red, but there are also shades of brown, grey, pink and green.

The canyon includes many smaller gorges and ravines, as well as interesting plants and wildlife. There are several kinds of trees, including ponderosa pine, juniper, aspen, fir and spruce. The cactus plant is also plentiful. Over 300 different species of birds have been spotted at the Grand Canyon. There are also elk, deer, mountain lions and several types of lizards and snakes, including the poisonous Grand Canyon pink rattlesnake, which is found nowhere else in the world.

Millions of people visit the Grand Canyon each year. Most are content to view the canyon from the rim, but some people hike or ride donkeys down to the bottom. Others choose to take a helicopter tour or raft through the canyon on the Colorado River.

Name _____

Physical features

Grand Canyon

A. Use the information on page 50 to help you answer the questions.

1. In what state is the Grand Canyon located? _____

2. How long is the Grand Canyon? _____

3. About how deep is the Grand Canyon? _____

4. What are three types of rock that can be found in the Grand Canyon?
   _____

5. In your own words, describe how the Grand Canyon was formed.
   _____
   _____

B. Pretend you are going to the bottom of the Grand Canyon. Answer the questions about how you will plan your trip. Use the information on page 50 to help you.

1. Will you hike, ride or raft to the bottom of the canyon? Why did you choose that way?
   _____
   _____

2. What are four things that you will need to bring with you?
   _____
   _____

3. Name two things you would like to see and do on a visit to the Grand Canyon.
   _____
   _____

Deserts of North America

There are four major deserts in North America. They are the Chihuahuan, Sonoran, Mojave and Great Basin deserts. These deserts are connected to each other and cover a large area of the south-western United States and Mexico.

Because these areas get very little rain—usually under 250 mm a year—plants must be hardy in order to survive. However, a surprising number of plants thrive in the desert environment, including sagebrush, creosote bush, agave, yucca and cactuses. These plants provide food and protection for many desert animals. Coyotes, jack rabbits, bighorn sheep, pocket mice, rattlesnakes, Gila monsters and roadrunners are a few of the animals that make the desert their home.

Even though all four of North America's major deserts are located in the south-western part of the continent, they are each different in size, climate and plant life. The climate of a desert is determined by where it is located on the continent and by its elevation, or height above sea level. Deserts that are further south and lower in elevation will be warmer. Deserts that are located further north and at higher elevations will be cooler.

The four deserts of North America

Desert	Size	Interesting facts
Chihuahuan	453 000 sq. km	This vast, mountainous desert is located on a high plateau. It is covered with stones and sandy soil. The number of different plants that grow in the Chihuahuan is not high. Yuccas, agave and cactuses are common.
Great Basin	492 000 sq. km	The Great Basin Desert is a cool desert because it is further north on the continent and because it is located at a high elevation. The terrain includes areas with mountains, as well as flat salt beds.
Mojave	65 000 sq. km	This desert includes Death Valley, where it gets extremely hot, as well as cooler areas further north. The Joshua tree can be found only in the Mojave. There are also many unique rock formations.
Sonoran	311 000 sq. km	Located far to the south and low in elevation, the Sonoran desert is the hottest of the North American deserts. The Sonoran also gets more rain than the other North American deserts.

Name _____

Physical features

Deserts of North America

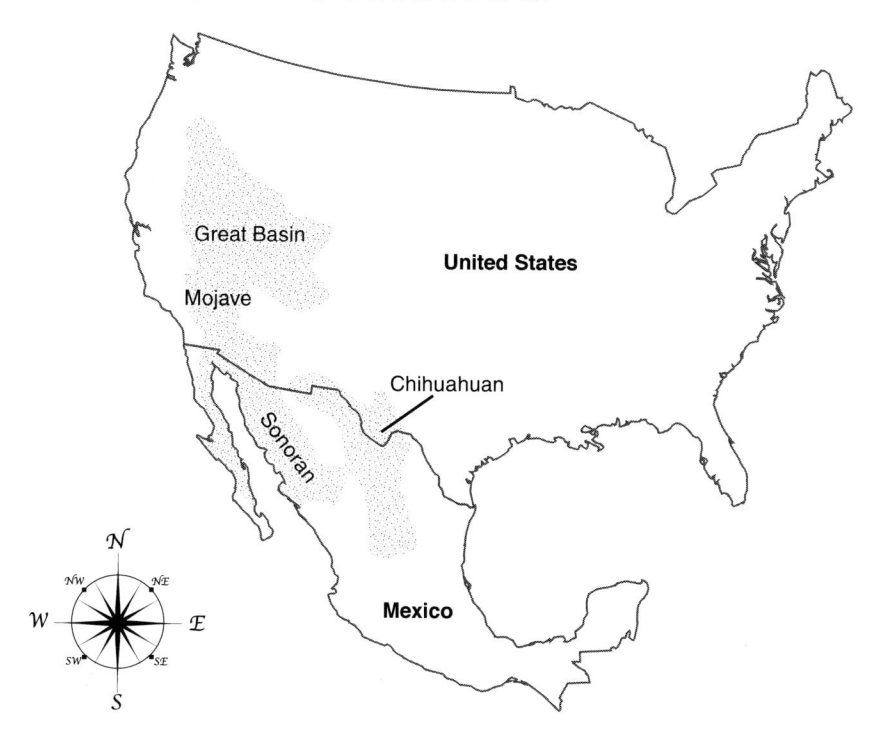

[Map of North America showing the following deserts: Great Basin, Mojave, Sonoran, and Chihuahuan, with the United States and Mexico labeled. A compass rose shows N, NE, E, SE, S, SW, W, NW.]

Circle the answer that completes each sentence. Use the information on page 52 to help you.

1.	The four major deserts are mostly in the ___.	south-west	south-east
2.	An agave is ___.	a plant	an animal
3.	An animal that lives in the desert is the ___.	lemming	pocket mouse
4.	The ___ is a cool desert.	Chihuahuan	Great Basin
5.	Death Valley is in the ___ Desert.	Mojave	Sonoran
6.	Joshua trees can be found in the ___.	Great Basin	Mojave
7.	The ___ is the hottest desert.	Chihuahuan	Sonoran
8.	The ___ is located on a plateau.	Chihuahuan	Mojave
9.	The ___ is the biggest desert.	Great Basin	Sonoran
10.	The ___ desert covers 311 000 sq km	Chihuahuan	Sonoran

Frozen north

The northern regions of North America are very cold. They stretch all the way into the Arctic Circle, which is an area that surrounds the North Pole. In the winter, temperatures in the northern part of the continent may reach as low as –50 °C. The land in the coldest regions of the north is called *tundra*, meaning that the ground there is permanently frozen. In this environment, no trees and only a few stout plants can grow. In the areas closest to the Arctic Circle, nothing grows at all.

Although the entire north is very cold, different regions of the north have different landscapes. Parts of Alaska and the north-western part of Canada are mountainous with many glaciers. Closer to Hudson Bay in the east, there are large coniferous forests. Conifers are trees such as pines, spruces, and firs that have needles for leaves. This type of landscape is called *taiga*, or *boreal forest*. The area has cold, snowy winters and short, warmer summers. Around the Hudson Bay there are also very rocky areas with many lakes. This area is called the Canadian Shield.

To the far north, the Arctic Islands are cold and barren. Some have mountains while others are flat. Many of these islands are unexplored. Greenland is the largest island in the world, but few people live there due to the harsh climate. About 80% of the island is covered in a 1.6 km-thick sheet of ice.

A. Use the information above to answer the questions.

1. What is a tundra?

   _____

   _____

2. What is a taiga?

   _____

   _____

3. Why don't many people live in Greenland?

   _____

   _____

Name _____

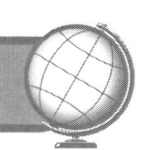

Physical features

Frozen north

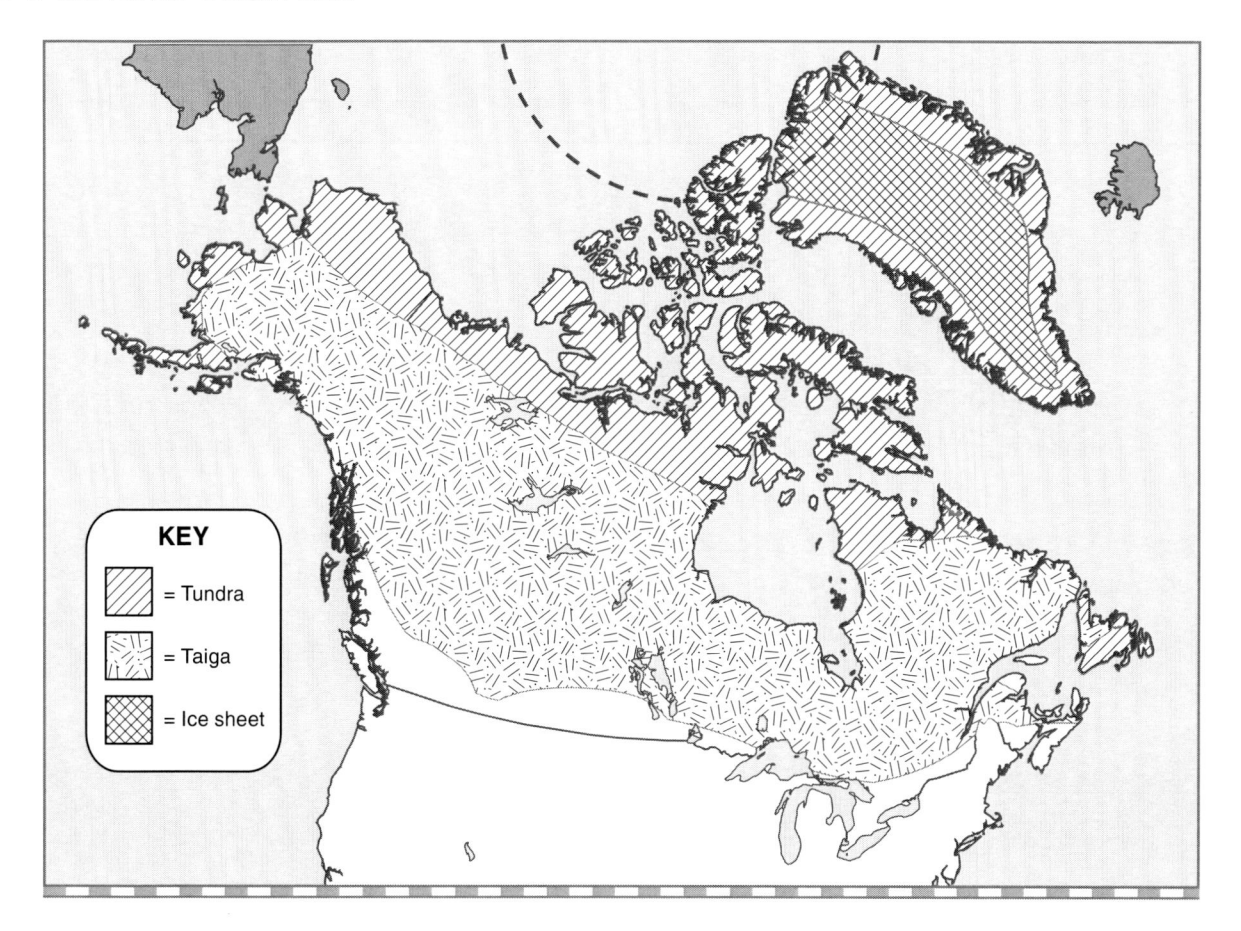

KEY
- ⧄ = Tundra
- ⦀ = Taiga
- ⊠ = Ice sheet

B. Follow the directions to colour the map.

1. Colour the taiga region green.
2. Colour the tundra purple.
3. Colour the ice sheet grey.
4. Use red to trace the dotted line (Arctic Circle).

Name _____

Physical features

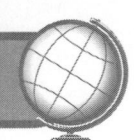

Central America's rainforests

Rainforests cover about 222 739 square km of Central America. That may seem like a lot but sadly, large areas of Central America's rainforests have been destroyed. El Salvador is the most deforested country in Central America, with 85% of its rainforest destroyed.

Rainforests in Central America have been destroyed for many reasons. Many have been logged for timber, both legally and illegally. In other areas, the land has been cleared to grow crops or to create pasture land for raising cattle. Some rainforests have also been destroyed by mining, road construction and forest fires.

Tropical rainforests are home to millions of plants and animals. In the tiny Central American country of Costa Rica alone, there are about 12 000 kinds of plants and 1200 kinds of butterflies! Unfortunately, many of these plants and animals are endangered as a result of illegal hunting and the loss of habitat.

Fortunately, some Central American rainforests are protected by the government. Environmental groups are working hard to save the others.

Central American rainforest

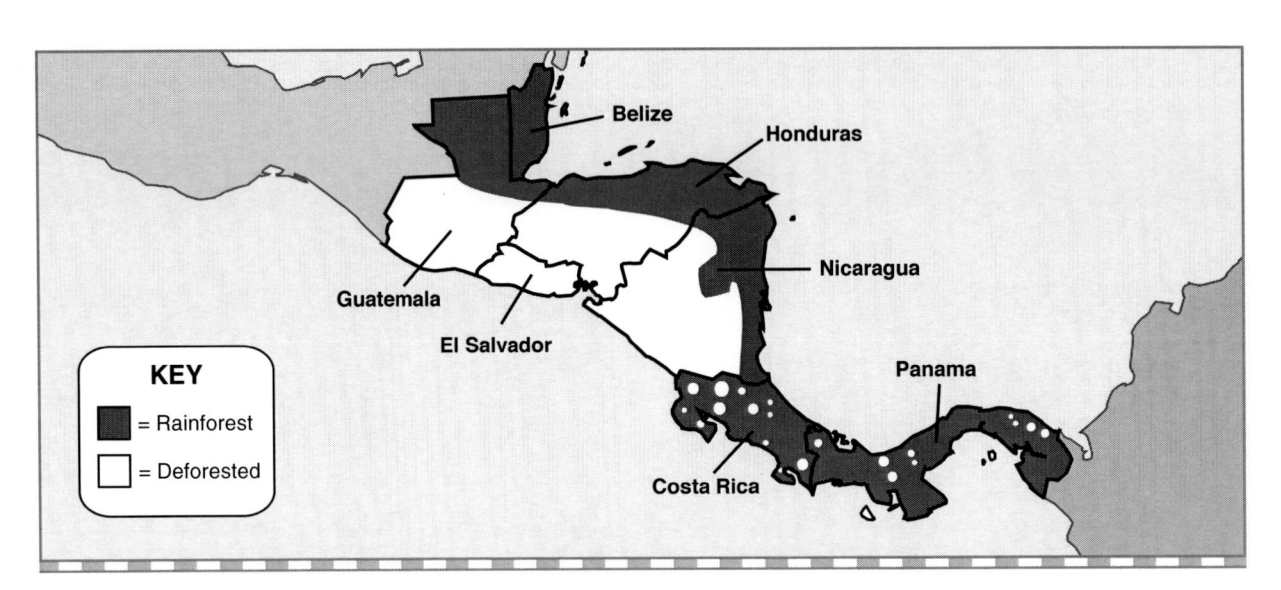

KEY
■ = Rainforest
□ = Deforested

A. Write four reasons why rainforests in Central America have been destroyed.

1. _____   3. _____

2. _____   4. _____

Central America's rainforests

B. Use the information page 56 to complete the secret code. Read each clue below and write the answer. Then use the numbers to crack the code!

1. Many of the tropical rainforests in Central America have been ____.

   ___ ___ ___ ___ ___ ___ ___ ___ ___
   10 11 25 26 24 21   5 11 10

2. El Salvador has lost 85 ____ of its rainforest.

   ___ ___ ___   ___ ___ ___ ___
   22 11 24   9 11 20 26

3. Trees are often cut down and logged for ____.

   ___ ___ ___ ___ ___ ___
   26 15 19   8 11 24

4. Many rainforests have been cleared to make ____ land for raising cattle.

   ___ ___ ___ ___ ___ ___ ___
   22   7 25 26   1 24 11

5. There are about 12 000 different ____ of plants in Costa Rica.

   ___ ___ ___ ___ ___
   17 15 20 10 25

6. Some Central American rainforests are protected by the ____.

   ___ ___ ___ ___ ___ ___ ___ ___ ___ ___
   14 21 23 11 24 20 19 11 20 26

Crack the code!

Several species of Central and South American ____ are endangered.

___ ___ ___ ___ ___ ___   ___ ___ ___ ___ ___ ___ ___
25 22 15 10 11 24   19 21 20 17 11   5 25

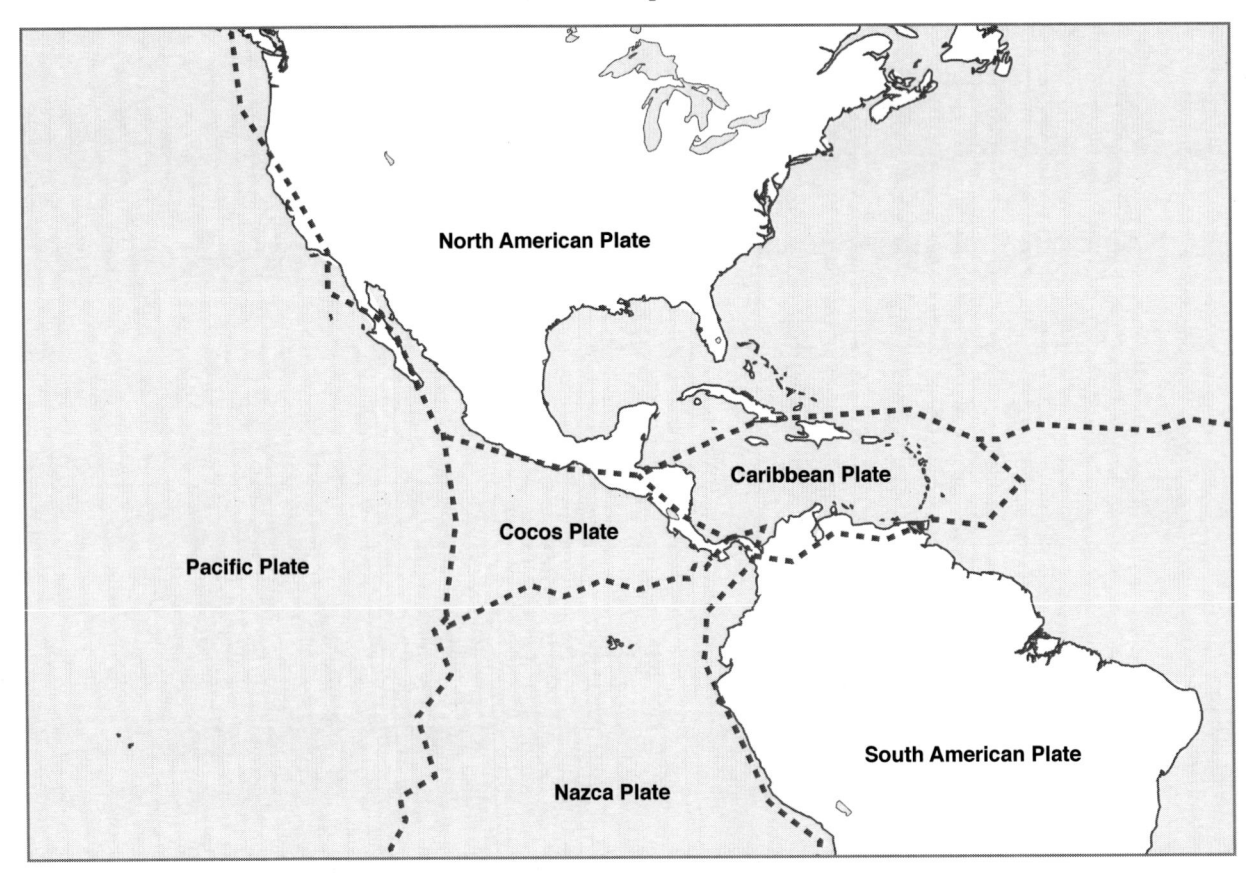

Islands of the Caribbean

The Caribbean Sea and the Atlantic Ocean are separated by a chain of islands called the Caribbean islands, or West Indies. This island chain is over 3200 km long and stretches from the tip of Florida to the northern coast of Venezuela in South America.

There are thousands of islands in the Caribbean island chain. The islands are part of an ancient underwater mountain range that stretched between North and South America. Many of the islands were once the peaks of mountains. Over millions of years, the peaks were worn away by the wind and rain. Other islands were formed when volcanoes erupted below the sea. There are still live volcanoes on several of the Caribbean islands.

The Caribbean islands are located over the intersection of several tectonic plates. Tectonic plates are large sections of Earth's crust. These massive plates move slowly into or away from each other, plunging the edge of one plate under the other, or ripping the crust apart. Movement of the tectonic plates often results in violent natural disasters, such as earthquakes, tsunamis (large ocean waves) and volcanic eruptions. Earthquakes and volcanic eruptions are still common on the Caribbean islands. For example, a 7.0 magnitude earthquake struck the Caribbean nation of Haiti in 2010, killing more than 200 000 people.

Tectonic plates

Name _____

Physical features

Islands of the Caribbean

Circle the answer that completes each sentence. Use information from page 58 and the chart of Caribbean volcanoes below to help you.

Volcano	Island	Last eruption
Soufrière Hills	Montserrat	2010
Soufrière Guadeloupe	Guadeloupe	1977
Morne Watt	Dominica	1997
Pelée	Martinique	1932
Qualibou	St Lucia	1766
Soufrière St Vincent	St Vincent	1979
Kick 'em Jenny	Grenada*	2001

*Located off the coast of Grenada

1. Some of the Caribbean islands were formed by ____.

   earthquakes   **tsunamis**   **volcanoes**

2. A tectonic plate is a large piece of the Earth's ____.

   crust   **continent**   **core**

3. Most of the Caribbean islands are on the Caribbean and ____ plates.

   South American   **North American**   **Cocos**

4. The most recent Caribbean volcanic eruption was on the island of ____.

   Dominica   **Grenada**   **Montserrat**

5. ____ Caribbean volcanoes have erupted in the last hundred years.

   Six   **Seven**   **Nine**

6. Kick 'em Jenny is near the island of ____.

   St Lucia   **Dominica**   **Grenada**

7. Qualibou erupted in ____.

   1766   **1979**   **1932**

Name _____

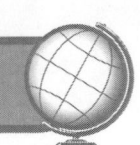

Physical features

North America's bodies of water

North America is bordered by three oceans. They are the Pacific, Atlantic and Arctic. However, there are also many seas, gulfs and bays that surround North America. For example, the Caribbean Sea is a part of the Atlantic Ocean that surrounds the Caribbean islands in south-eastern North America. The Gulf of California is a small sliver of the Pacific Ocean that separates Baja California from mainland Mexico. And the Hudson Bay is a portion of the northern Atlantic Ocean that cuts into Canada.

North America also contains several long rivers and large lakes. The Mississippi River system in the United States is one of the largest river systems in the world. It includes the Mississippi, Missouri and Ohio rivers. Lake Superior, one of the Great Lakes that separate the US and Canada, is the largest freshwater lake on the planet.

A. Look at the map on page 61. Match each body of water below to the corresponding number on the map. Then label the body of water on the map.

1. Arctic Ocean
2. Atlantic Ocean
3. Pacific Ocean
4. Gulf of Mexico
5. Gulf of California
6. Caribbean Sea
7. Hudson Bay
8. Lake Superior

B. Use the information above and the map on page 61 to answer the questions.

1. Which bay is furthest north? _____

2. Which body of water separates two areas of Mexico? _____

3. What ocean is the Caribbean Sea connected to? _____

4. What is the northern-most gulf in the United States? _____

5. Which bay separates Canada and Greenland? _____

Name _____

Physical features

North America's bodies of water

Name _____

Physical features

Great Lakes

The Great Lakes are located on the border between Canada and the United States. Of the five lakes, only Lake Michigan is completely within the United States. The other four lakes help form the border between the United States and Canada.

The Great Lakes were formed during the last ice age, about 10 000 years ago. Huge sheets of ice, called glaciers, covered Canada and the northern United States. When the glaciers receded, they left ridges and large basins. Some of the water from the melting glaciers filled in these basins, creating the lakes.

The Great Lakes and the channels that connect them form the largest freshwater system on Earth. They hold about one-fifth of the world's supply of fresh water. If the water from the Great Lakes was spread evenly over the United States (not including Alaska and Hawaii), the entire country would be covered in 3 metres of water!

Lake Superior is the largest and deepest of the Great Lakes. It is also the coldest lake. Lake Ontario is the smallest lake, but it actually contains four times as much water as Lake Erie, which is about 6700 square kilometres larger than Lake Ontario. That is because Lake Erie is very shallow. Since it is so shallow, Lake Erie warms up quickly in summer. It is more likely to freeze in winter than the other Great Lakes.

The five Great Lakes

Great Lake	Size	Average depth	Maximum depth
Erie	25 700 sq km	19 m	64 m
Huron	59 600 sq km	59 m	229 m
Michigan	57 800 sq km	85 m	282 m
Ontario	19 000 sq km	86 m	244 m
Superior	82 100 sq km	147 m	406 m

A. Write a caption for the map on page 63 to compare at least two of the lakes. Use the information on this page to help you.

_____
_____
_____
_____

Name _____

Physical features

Great Lakes

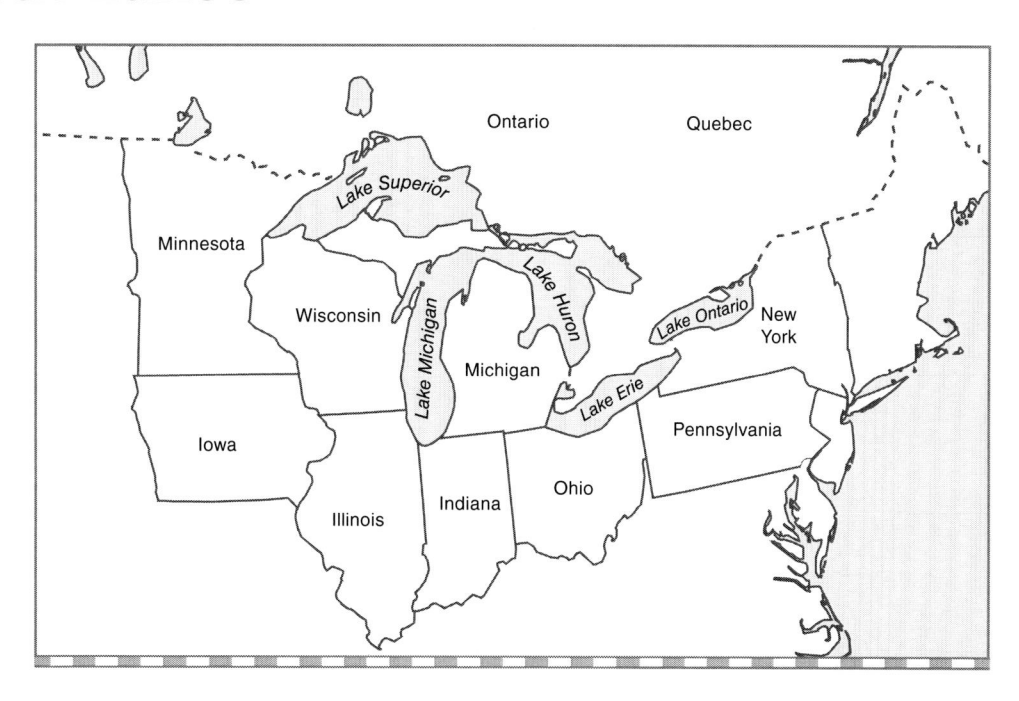

_____

_____

B. Circle the lake that matches each clue. Use the information on page 62 and the map above to help you.

1. the largest lake — **Lake Superior**   **Lake Michigan**
2. the shallowest lake — **Lake Erie**   **Lake Ontario**
3. the smallest lake — **Lake Erie**   **Lake Ontario**
4. the second-largest lake — **Lake Michigan**   **Lake Huron**
5. the only lake completely in the US — **Lake Michigan**   **Lake Huron**
6. the coldest lake — **Lake Ontario**   **Lake Superior**
7. the lake with an average depth of 86 metres — **Lake Erie**   **Lake Ontario**
8. the lake that has an area of 57 800 square kilometres — **Lake Superior**   **Lake Michigan**

Name _____

Physical features

North America's rivers

There are hundreds of rivers in North America. Rivers are an important source of fresh water. Farmers use rivers to irrigate crops. Rivers provide important transportation routes for goods and people. Rivers can also be used to produce hydroelectricity, which is electricity that is produced by the energy of running water.

The Missouri River is the longest river in North America. It is 4023 km long. The Missouri River and the Ohio River are tributaries of the mighty Mississippi River. That means that they flow into the Mississippi. Together, these three rivers make up the third-largest river system in the world.

In Canada, the St Lawrence River connects the Great Lakes to the Atlantic Ocean. It is an important waterway for transporting goods.

The Rio Grande River forms most of the border between Texas and Mexico. And in Central America, the longest river is the Rio Coco. It forms much of the boundary between Honduras and Nicaragua.

A. This map shows 12 major rivers in North America. Write the numbers **1** to **5** to label the five longest rivers in order from longest to shortest. Use the chart on page 65 to help you.

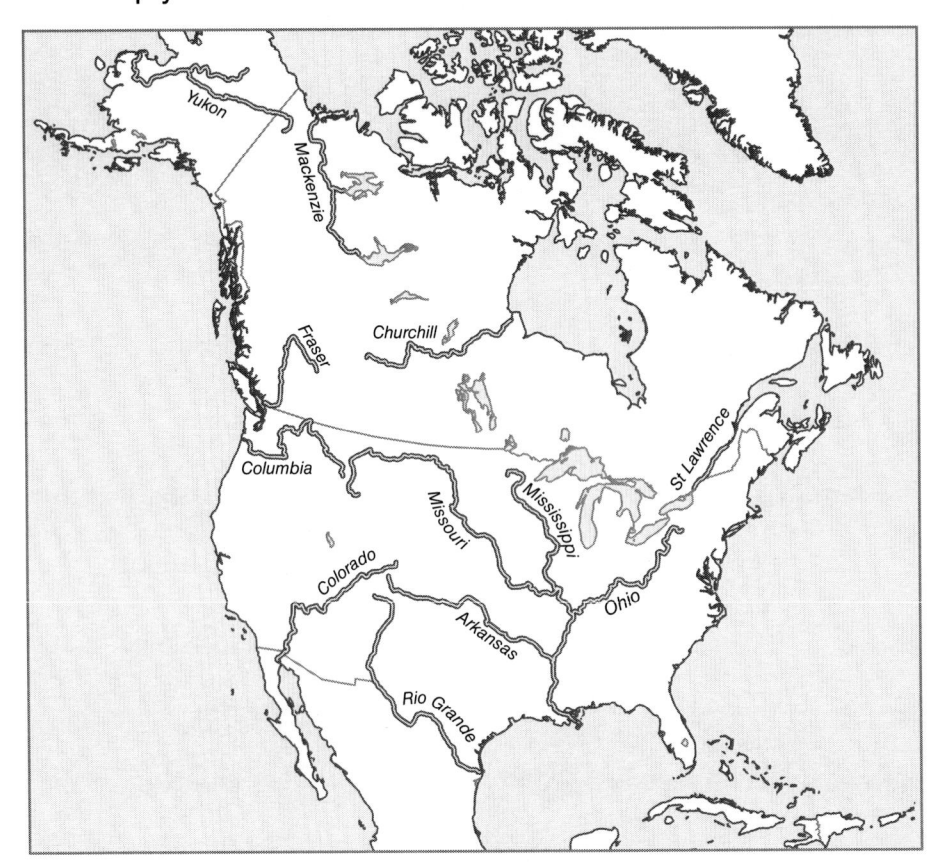

Name _____

Physical features

North America's rivers

River	Length in kilometres
Arkansas	2350 km
Churchill	1609 km
Colorado	2333 km
Columbia	1854 km
Fraser	1368 km
Mackenzie	1931 km
Mississippi	3765 km
Missouri	4023 km
Ohio	1569 km
Rio Grande	3034 km
St Lawrence	1223 km
Yukon	2036 km

B. In the word puzzle, find and circle the names of the rivers from above. Words may appear across, down or diagonally.

```
F C O L O R A D O Y P E L R E
S O R A T J M E W F A D Q U I
T L I R X M L A L P R N A B N
L U C K E I Z N E K I A M Z C
A M O A A S B S L I O R S O H
W B R N T S A V R B G G M E U
R I W S E I Q U U M R O M L R
E A O A C S O U L K A I R E C
N R T S A S M O L Z N R M C H
C E V O S I R U O S D I M P I
E Z I I K P B N S H E E P X L
A H M N I P N Y U K O N L M L
O K H O T I M A C K E N Z I E
```

www.prim-ed.com Prim-Ed Publishing Exploring geography: North America 65

Name _____

Physical features

Panama Canal

The Panama Canal was one of the most ambitious building projects in human history. It was cut through the narrowest part of Central America to connect the Pacific and Atlantic oceans. Before the construction of the canal in 1914, ships had to sail all the way around South America. That meant an extra 12 800 km for a ship to sail from New York to San Francisco.

The canal is 82 km long and up to 16 km wide. It takes nine hours to make the crossing. The reason it takes so long is that the canal was cut through land that is about 26 metres above sea level. So ships must be raised up to this level when they enter the canal, and lowered back down when they exit. This is done with a series of locks, or sections of water with gates between them. When the gates are opened or closed, water flows in or out, raising and lowering the boat on the water. About 40 ships cross each day; that's about 14 000 ships each year.

Facts about the Panama Canal

- France was the first country to attempt building the canal in the late 1800s. The French failed, and nearly 20 000 workers lost their lives, most to tropical diseases such as yellow fever and malaria.
- The workers who built the canal had to deal with huge swarms of insects, including mosquitoes that carried dangerous diseases.
- The Panama Canal was finally built by the United States. It took 100 000 workers 11 years to build the canal.
- The official opening of the canal was on 15 August 1914. The *SS Ancon* was the first ship to sail through the canal.
- Although the canal was built by the United States, ownership was returned to Panama in 1999.
- The Panama Canal cost US $375 000 000 to build. That is equivalent to US $7 500 000 000 today.
- The gates between the locks have to be strong enough to hold back millions of litres of water. They are made of steel and are 2 m thick. Each of the hinges weighs over 12.7 tonnes.
- About 5% of the world's trade goods travel through the Panama Canal.
- Ships must pay a fee to use the canal. An average-sized cargo ship pays about US $43 000.

Name _____

Physical features

Panama Canal

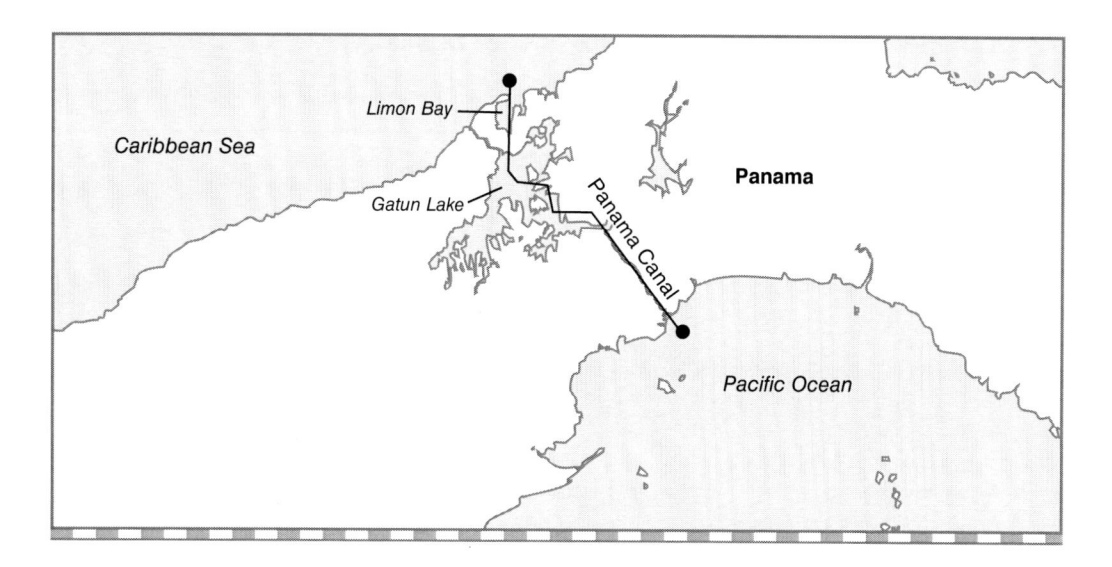

Unscramble the word below each line to complete the sentence. Use the information on page 66 to help you.

Some of the answers will need to start with capital letters.

1. The Panama Canal connects the Pacific and _____ oceans.
   ticlanat

2. The Panama Canal is up to 16 km _____.
   dwie

3. It took _____ years to build the canal.
   veenel

4. Workers built a series of _____ to lift ships above sea level.
   scolk

5. The _____ for the gates of the locks each weigh over 12 tonnes.
   sheign

6. The first attempt to build the canal was made by _____.
   cenfar

7. The Panama Canal officially opened on 15 _____ 1914.
   stugua

8. The SS _____ was the first ship through the Panama Canal.
   conan

www.prim-ed.com   Prim-Ed Publishing   Exploring geography: North America   67

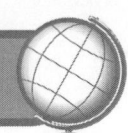

Review

Use words from the box to complete the crossword puzzle.

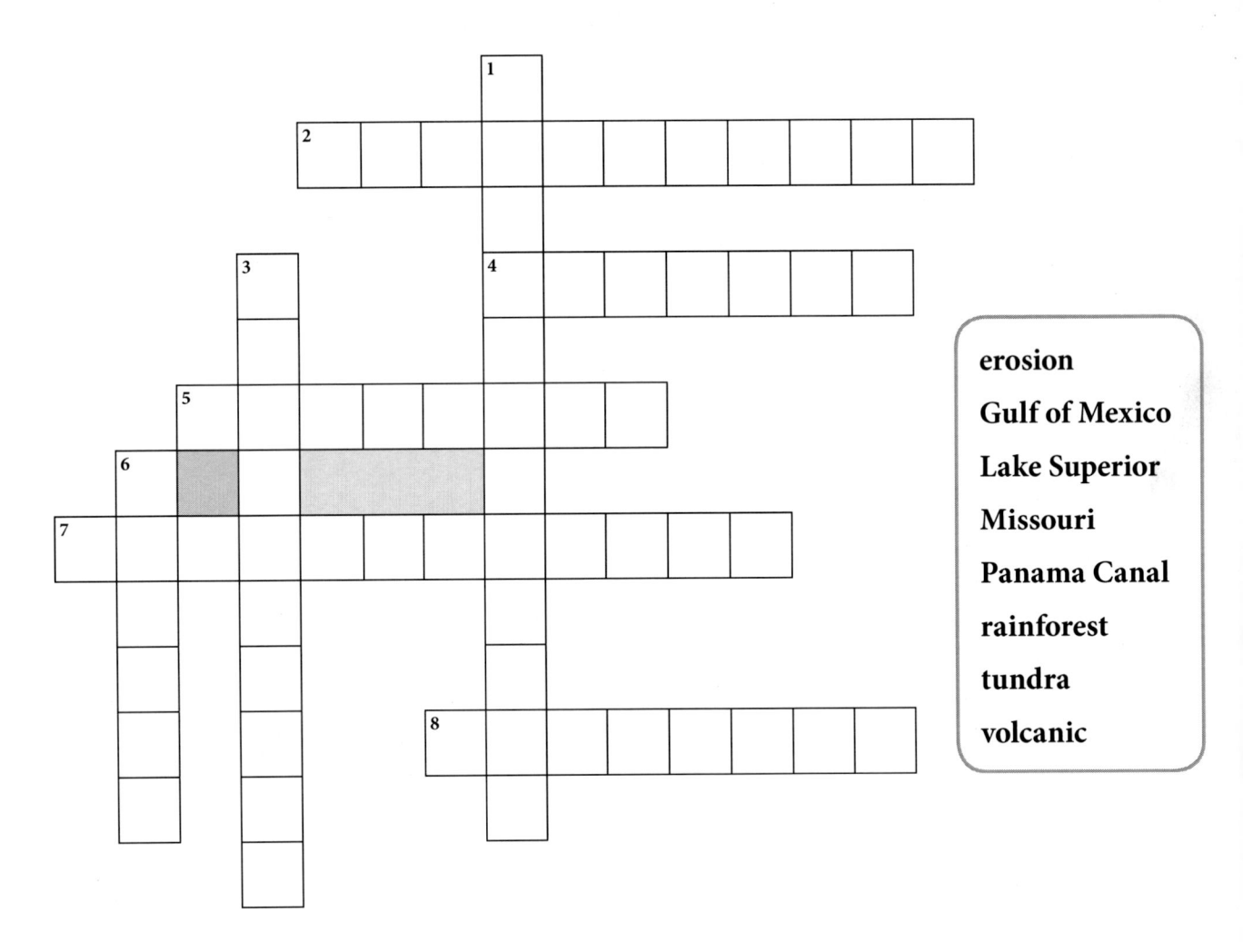

Word box:
- erosion
- Gulf of Mexico
- Lake Superior
- Missouri
- Panama Canal
- rainforest
- tundra
- volcanic

Across

2. an important waterway linking the Atlantic and the Pacific oceans
4. the process that formed the Grand Canyon
5. the longest river in North America
7. the body of water connected to the Caribbean Sea
8. Some Caribbean islands are ___.

Down

1. the largest of the Great Lakes
3. a region of dense vegetation
6. frozen land in the north

SECTION 4

Valuable resources of North America

In this section, pupils learn about the various natural resources of North America. They discover that energy production is an important industry on the continent. Pupils also learn about important regional crops and are introduced to some of the challenges of fishing and logging. In addition, they learn about interesting animals of North America.

CONTENTS

Overview 70–71	Coffee and bananas 82–83
Fossil fuels. 72–73	North America's forests 84–85
Hydroelectricity 74–75	Wildlife of North America. . . . 86–89
Renewable energy. 76–77	Review. .90
Fishing. 78–79	
Corn and livestock. 80–81	

Name _____

Valuable resources

Overview

Natural resources are materials found in nature that people can use. North America is rich in many kinds of natural resources. There are large deposits of fossil fuels, areas of ideal farming soil, abundant fish in the oceans and extensive forests teeming with plants and animals.

Energy

Oil, natural gas and coal are important resources in North America. These are all fossil fuels, which take millions of years to form and cannot be replaced. They also cause pollution when burned. Other less-polluting energy resources such as hydropower, wind power and solar power can never run out, so they are starting to replace the use of some of North America's fossil fuels.

Fishing and farming

Many people in the coastal communities of North America rely on fishing for their livelihood. Because fish is not a main food source for most North Americans, much of the catch is sent to other countries. However, the fish population of North America's waters has been decreasing significantly due to overfishing.

North America also grows much of the world's supply of corn, soybeans, wheat, coffee and bananas. Most farms in North America are very large, and many specialise in just one crop.

Forests

Most of Canada and parts of the west coast of the United States are covered by coniferous, or evergreen, forests. Other forests of trees such as maple, oak and birch cover the eastern part of the United States. There are also tropical forests in the southern parts of the continent. These forests are home to many species of plants and animals. However, many of these forests are being cut down for timber or to make room for croplands and pastures for grazing animals.

Animals

Many wild animals live in North America. Musk oxen and polar bears have thick coats to survive in the cold climate of the northern part of the continent, while humpback whales swim in the freezing Arctic Ocean. The milder climate in the middle of the continent provides the perfect environment for many kinds of mammals, from bison to beavers. Further south, desert lizards such as the Gila monster thrive in the hot sun, while birds such as the colourful Central American quetzal make their home in the tropical rainforest.

Name _____

Valuable resources

Overview

Tick the box to answer each question or complete each sentence.

1. Which of these resources is *not* a fossil fuel?
   - ☐ coal
   - ☐ natural gas
   - ☐ wind
   - ☐ oil

2. Which of these crops was *not* mentioned in the information on the other page?
   - ☐ bananas
   - ☐ olives
   - ☐ soybeans
   - ☐ corn

3. Most of Canada is covered by ____.
   - ☐ coniferous forests
   - ☐ rainforests
   - ☐ mountains
   - ☐ deserts

4. Which of these animals lives in a hot climate?
   - ☐ musk ox
   - ☐ Gila monster
   - ☐ humpback whale
   - ☐ bison

5. Which of these animals lives in the tropical rainforest?
   - ☐ beaver
   - ☐ Gila monster
   - ☐ bison
   - ☐ quetzal

Name _____

Valuable resources

Fossil fuels

North America is rich in oil, natural gas and coal. These are all types of fossil fuels. Fossil fuels were formed from the remains of animals and plants that lived millions of years ago. Fossil fuels are non-renewable, meaning they cannot be replaced once they're used up because they take millions of years to form. Over half the energy that the United States and Canada use comes from fossil fuels.

Oil and natural gas are found in large underground deposits and are reached by drilling. Oil is used to make petrol, diesel fuel and heating oil. Natural gas is used mainly to heat buildings and for cooking.

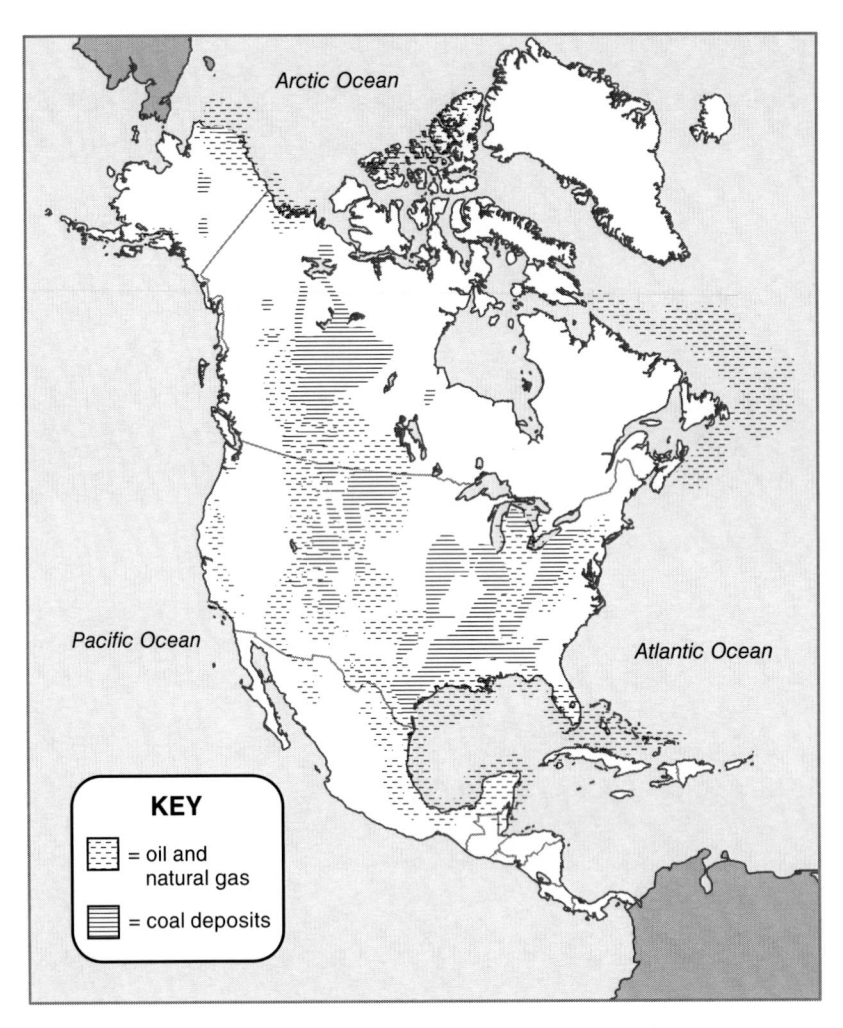

KEY
▨ = oil and natural gas
☰ = coal deposits

Coal is a mineral that is mined using heavy machinery and explosives. It is burned to make electricity and to heat buildings. Unfortunately, burning coal, as well as oil and natural gas, causes pollution that some scientists believe is contributing to global warming. The process of removing coal from the ground can also cause a lot of damage to the environment.

Deposits of oil, natural gas and coal tend to be found in the same area. There is a great deal of coal in the Appalachian Mountains in the eastern United States and south-west of the Great Lakes. Natural gas can be found in the Gulf of Mexico area, as well as south-east of the Great Lakes. Large oil fields are found off the coast of Alaska and in California, Texas, and Mexico.

Name _____

Valuable resources

Fossil fuels

A. Read each statement. Circle **yes** if it is true or **no** if it is false. Use the information on page 72 to help you.

1. Oil, natural gas and coal are fossil fuels.   Yes   No

2. North America will never run out of coal.   Yes   No

3. Half the energy used in the US comes from natural gas.   Yes   No

4. Natural gas is used to heat buildings and for cooking.   Yes   No

5. Coal mining does not do much damage to the land.   Yes   No

6. Fossil fuels cause pollution.   Yes   No

7. Fossil fuels take millions of years to form.   Yes   No

8. People use explosives to find oil.   Yes   No

9. Coal is burned to make electricity.   Yes   No

10. People use oil to make petrol and diesel fuel.   Yes   No

B. What are two problems associated with using coal for fuel?

1. _____

2. _____

C. Use the map on page 72 to help you answer the questions.

1. Which part of the United States has more coal, _____
eastern or western?

2. In which two oceans are there large deposits of oil and natural gas?

_____

www.prim-ed.com   Prim-Ed Publishing   Exploring geography: North America   **73**

Name _____

Valuable resources

Hydroelectricity

The rivers of North America provide an important resource. Water from rivers can be used to generate electricity. This form of energy is called *hydroelectricity*. Hydroelectricity is a renewable resource and is relatively inexpensive to produce. Also, unlike burning fossil fuels, hydroelectricity does not cause pollution.

In order to use water to make electricity, people must construct a dam on a river. A single river may have hundreds of dams along its length. Unfortunately, that can have some negative effects on the environment. Damming a river makes it impossible for migrating fish such as salmon to swim up the river to lay their eggs. It also makes the water warmer, which is not good for plants and animals that are adapted to colder temperatures. In addition, dams cause a build-up of mud and silt, which can clog a river.

About 15% of the world's electricity comes from hydroelectricity. Rivers in the Canadian Shield provide a great deal of hydroelectricity in Quebec and Ontario. The United States has over 2000 hydroelectric plants. Of these, the Grand Coulee Dam on the Columbia River in Washington produces the most electricity.

Hydroelectricity uses the power of flowing water to create electricity. Here's how it works:

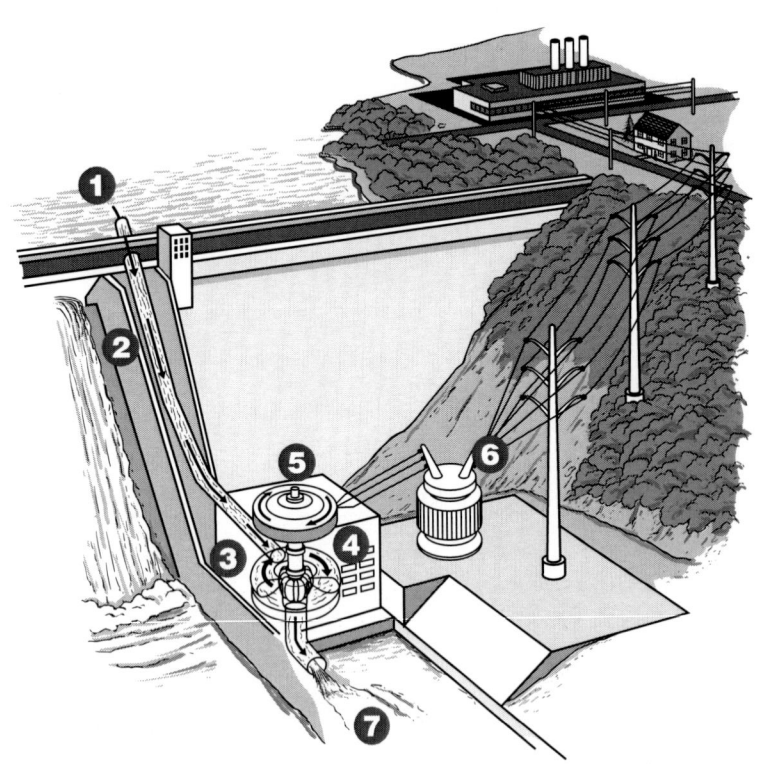

1. Water from behind the dam falls through the floodgates.
2. The water gathers speed as it flows down through a tunnel called a *penstock*.
3. The water hits the blades of a machine called a *turbine*, causing the turbine to spin quickly.
4. The turbine is attached to a shaft. As the turbine spins, so does the shaft.
5. The shaft spins magnets in the generator. This makes electricity in the wire coils that surround the magnets.
6. The electricity is carried away to homes and buildings by the transmission wires.
7. The water flows out of the dam and down the river.

Name _____

Valuable resources

Hydroelectricity

A. Number the steps for making hydroelectricity in order from **1** to **7**.
Use the diagram on page 74 to help you.

_____ The water hits the blades of the turbine, making the turbine spin.

_____ The water flows out of the dam and down the river.

_____ Electricity is carried away by the transmission wires.

_____ The shaft spins magnets in the generator to make electricity.

_____ Water comes through the floodgates.

_____ The shaft spins.

_____ The water flows down through the penstock.

B. What are three environmental problems that are caused by dams?

1. _____

2. _____

3. _____

C. What are three advantages of using hydroelectricity?

1. _____

2. _____

3. _____

Name _____

Valuable resources

Renewable energy

In addition to hydroelectricity, there are several other sources of renewable energy used in North America. Two of the most important sources of renewable energy are the sun and the wind.

Solar power

Solar power is energy that we get from the sun in the form of heat and light.

Solar power that can be used to heat water is called *solar thermal power*. In North America, the most common use of solar thermal power is for heating swimming pools. The first solar thermal power plant was built in the Mojave Desert in 1984.

Solar panels

Even though this project was a success, few solar thermal plants have been built since.

Solar power can also be used to create electrical energy. Solar panels collect light and turn it into electricity that can be used in homes and businesses. Large systems can even generate enough electricity to meet the needs of entire cities. However, although sunlight is free, ways of collecting and converting it to electricity are still very expensive, so there are not many large solar power plants in North America. Some of the largest solar plants are located in Ontario, Canada, and in Nevada and California in the US.

Wind power

The same wind that lifts a kite into the air can also generate electricity for thousands of homes. People collect the power of the wind using *wind turbines*.

Wind turbines are huge towers with giant blades that are spun by the wind. The spinning turbines power generators that make electricity.

Wind turbines

When many wind turbines are built together in one place, they are called a *wind farm*. Wind farms are built in places that get a lot of wind.

In North America, the vast majority of wind farms are found in the United States. However, there are some in Canada and Mexico as well.

The largest wind farm in the world has 627 turbines and is located in Texas. This wind farm makes enough electricity to power over 230 000 homes!

Name _____

Valuable resources

Renewable energy

A. Find and circle the solar and wind power words in the word puzzle. Words may appear across, down or diagonally.

E	C	O	L	L	E	C	T	B	V	H	T	H	E
N	G	N	M	O	Z	E	T	N	E	K	G	T	L
E	R	X	R	M	W	P	O	A	J	Y	E	U	E
R	S	P	E	C	O	N	V	E	R	T	M	R	C
G	W	I	N	D	F	A	R	M	W	Y	I	B	T
Y	H	R	E	I	M	A	T	A	S	Y	B	I	R
E	S	E	W	U	M	G	T	B	E	A	R	N	I
S	O	L	A	R	P	A	N	E	L	T	U	E	C
R	R	T	B	I	E	M	H	E	R	A	T	O	I
N	O	H	L	H	W	S	U	O	Y	O	D	H	T
D	Q	G	E	N	E	R	A	T	O	R	U	E	Y
E	G	E	H	T	E	T	U	C	O	S	Y	A	S

blades
collect
convert
electricity
energy
generator
heat
renewable
solar panel
turbine
wind farm

B. Choose three words from the word box and write a sentence using each word. Underline the words you used from the box.

1. _____

2. _____

3. _____

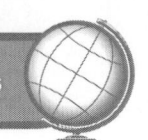

Fishing

Fishing is a big industry in the coastal areas of North America. Many people depend on fishing to earn a living. Canada, the sixth-largest exporter of fish in the world, brings in more than US $2 000 000 000 each year from selling fish. The United States is the world's third-largest seafood producer and, like Canada, also exports much of the fish it catches. Mexico also ranks in the top 20 seafood producers in the world.

The largest fishing zone in North America is in the North Atlantic Ocean. About 25% of the world's fish comes from this area, which stretches from Newfoundland in Canada to New England in the north-eastern United States. Another large fishing area is located in the Pacific Ocean, along the coasts of California, Oregon, Washington, British Columbia and Alaska.

People once thought the supply of fish was endless. But in recent years there have been disturbing signs that many species of fish are declining. Wild salmon are just one example of a threatened species.

Wild Alaskan sockeye salmon

North American salmon live along the Pacific coast from Alaska to California. In the wild, salmon are born in freshwater streams and rivers. They make their way downstream to the ocean, where they spend most of their lives. When they are ready to breed, they swim upstream in order to return to the same place where they were spawned, or hatched. Over the last several decades, there has been a sharp decrease in the wild salmon population. Pollution, dams, overfishing and other human activities have contributed to this decline.

In order to meet the demand for salmon as a food, the industry of salmon farming has grown. Farmed salmon live in large underwater cages in the ocean. These cages are usually made of mesh and framed by steel. Each cage can hold up to 90 000 fish and keeps the fish safe from potential predators. However, there are concerns that farmed salmon are also contributing to the declining populations of wild salmon. Escaped farmed salmon can spread diseases and parasites to the wild salmon population. They can also breed with the wild salmon and reduce the chances of their offspring surviving.

Name _____

Valuable resources

Fishing

A. Look at the map. Circle the names of the seafood that you have eaten. Draw a star next to the one you liked best.

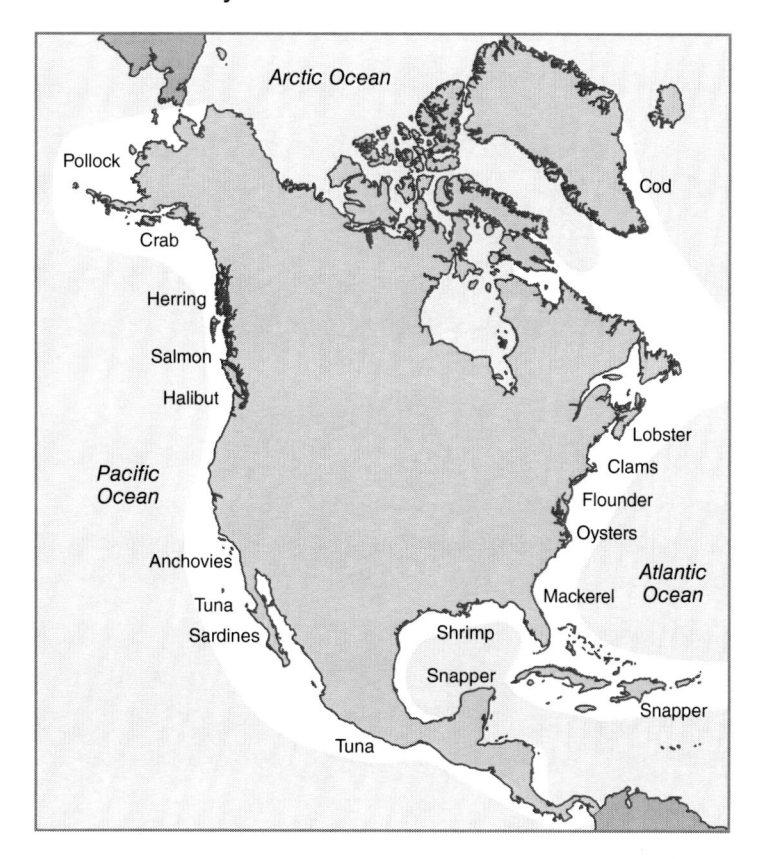

Arctic Ocean

Pollock
Cod
Crab
Herring
Salmon
Halibut
Lobster
Clams
Pacific Ocean
Flounder
Oysters
Anchovies
Mackerel *Atlantic Ocean*
Tuna
Sardines
Shrimp
Snapper
Snapper
Tuna

B. Use the information on page 78 to help you answer the questions.

1. Where is the largest fishing zone in North America? _____

2. Which country is the sixth-largest exporter of fish? _____

3. What are three human activities that have contributed to the decline of wild salmon?

   _____

4. What negative effects have farmed salmon had on the wild salmon population?

   _____

   _____

Corn and livestock

Although many kinds of crops are grown in North America, corn is one of the biggest. Most of the corn crop is used to feed livestock, such as cattle. Cattle are the most common type of livestock in North America and are raised for both beef and milk.

Corn

In North America, corn is grown from the southern parts of Canada down to Mexico. The vast majority of corn crops are grown in the midwestern United States. The US produces half the world's corn supply.

About 80% of the corn grown in the United States is used for animal feed. Another 12% is eaten by people. Some of this is in the form of fresh, tinned or frozen corn, and some is in products such as corn crisps or tortillas.

Corn is also used to make a sweetener called high fructose corn syrup. This is used in many shop-bought foods because it is inexpensive and helps the foods stay fresh longer. However, many doctors are concerned about the negative effects of high fructose corn syrup. Eating large amounts of it over a long period of time has been linked with gaining too much weight and developing diabetes, high blood pressure and heart disease.

Corn is also used to make ethanol, a type of fuel that can be used to run cars. Unlike petrol, ethanol is a renewable resource. However, it takes a great deal of land and processing to make ethanol, and it still causes pollution when it is burnt as fuel.

Livestock

Although cattle are raised in Canada, Mexico and Central America, the majority of cattle are raised in the midwestern and southern regions of the United States. With about 95 million cattle, the United States produces more beef than any other country.

Most beef cattle are raised on special areas called feedlots. They are fed mostly corn for about 140 days, at which time they are ready for the abattoir. About 40% of the beef produced in the US comes from large feedlots with over 32 000 animals.

Cows are also raised for milk production. Dairy cows are raised in all 50 states of the US, but the top milk-producing states are California, Wisconsin, New York and Idaho. Milk is also made into cheese, yoghurt, butter, ice-cream and other dairy products.

The United States also raises more chickens and turkeys than any other country. In addition, the US is a leading producer of eggs, with over 90 *billion* eggs produced each year!

Name _____

Valuable resources

Corn and livestock

Use the information on page 80 to crack the secret code. Read each clue below and write the correct word on the lines. Then use the numbers to crack the code!

1. The United States produces _____ of the world's supply of corn.

   $\overline{22}\ \overline{15}\ \overline{26}\ \overline{20}$

2. About 80% of the _____ grown in the United States is used to feed livestock.

   $\overline{17}\ \overline{3}\ \overline{6}\ \overline{2}$

3. Corn can be used to make a fuel source called _____.

   $\overline{19}\ \overline{8}\ \overline{22}\ \overline{15}\ \overline{2}\ \overline{3}\ \overline{26}$

4. Most beef cattle are raised in _____.

   $\overline{20}\ \overline{19}\ \overline{19}\ \overline{18}\ \overline{26}\ \overline{3}\ \overline{8}\ \overline{7}$

5. The state of _____ is one of the top producers of dairy products.

   $\overline{17}\ \overline{15}\ \overline{26}\ \overline{23}\ \overline{20}\ \overline{3}\ \overline{6}\ \overline{2}\ \overline{23}\ \overline{15}$

6. The United States produces more chickens and _____ than any other country.

   $\overline{8}\ \overline{9}\ \overline{6}\ \overline{25}\ \overline{19}\ \overline{13}\ \overline{7}$

Crack the code!

_____ are the most common breed of dairy cow in the United States because they produce the most milk.

$\overline{22}\ \overline{3}\ \overline{26}\ \overline{7}\ \overline{8}\ \overline{19}\ \overline{23}\ \overline{2}\ \overline{7}$

Name _____

Valuable resources

Coffee and bananas

Mexico and the seven countries of Central America grow a lot of coffee and bananas. In fact, Central America produces 10% of the world's supply of both bananas and coffee. Bananas are grown in the tropical lowlands, while coffee thrives in the highlands.

Banana tree   *Coffee plant*

Coffee and banana production in Mexico and Central America

Country	Tonnes of bananas per year	Tonnes of coffee per year
Belize	68 053	45
Costa Rica	1 881 783	107 258
El Salvador	65 000	97 727
Guatemala	1 569 460	254 800
Honduras	909 999	217 951
Mexico	1 782 205	243 910
Nicaragua	36 284	72 727
Panama	357 860	12 960

Food and Agriculture Organisation of the United Nations

A. Use the information from the chart to answer the questions.

1. Together, the three largest banana producers grow about how many tonnes of bananas yearly?

   less than 1 million tonnes   **almost 5 million tonnes**   **over 5 million tonnes**

2. Together, the three largest coffee producers grow about how many tonnes of coffee yearly?

   over 7 million tonnes   **over 700 000 tonnes**   **less than 70 000 tonnes**

Name _____

Valuable resources

Coffee and bananas

B. Circle the answer that completes each sentence. Use the chart on page 82 to help you.

Some of the answers will need to start with capital letters.

1. Mexico grows nearly 2 million tonnes of ___.	**coffee**	**bananas**
2. Coffee is grown in the ___.	**highlands**	**lowlands**
3. ___ produces the most bananas.	**Guatemala**	**Costa Rica**
4. ___ produces the most coffee.	**Guatemala**	**Costa Rica**
5. Honduras produces more ___.	**coffee**	**bananas**
6. El Salvador produces more ___.	**coffee**	**bananas**

C. Look at the map of Mexico and Central America below. Number the countries from **1** to **8** according to how many tonnes of bananas they produce each year.

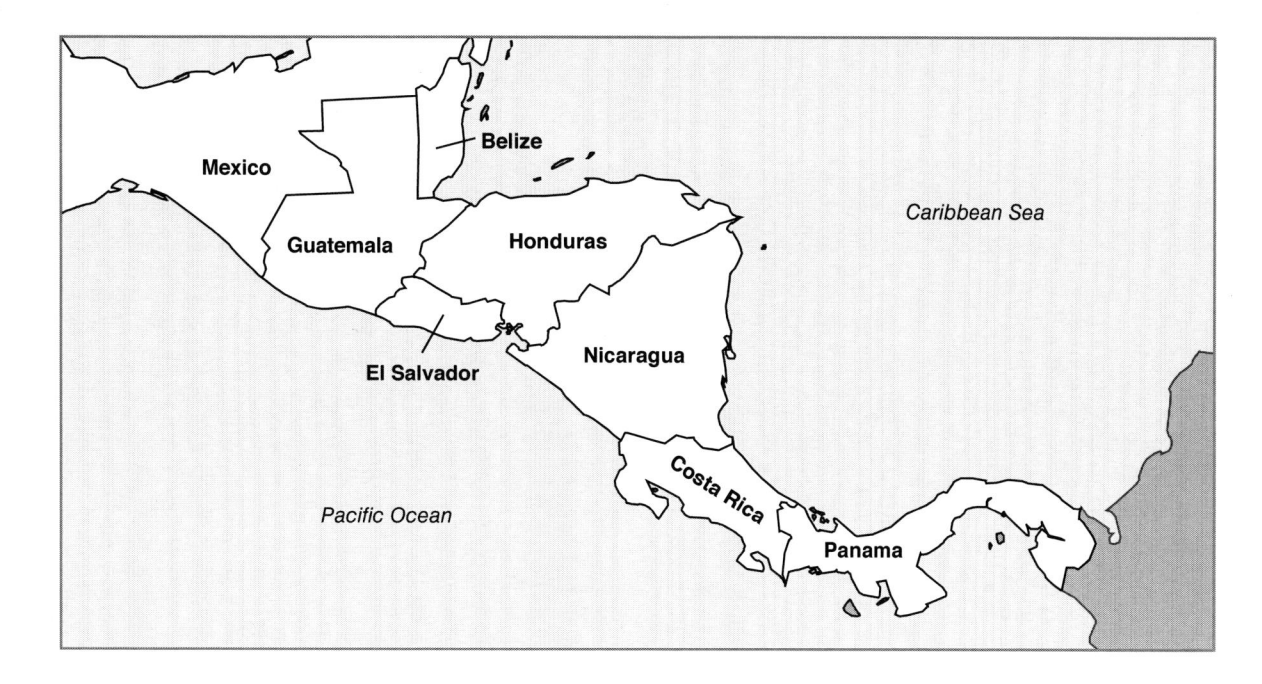

[Map of Mexico and Central America showing: Mexico, Belize, Guatemala, Honduras, El Salvador, Nicaragua, Costa Rica, Panama, with the Caribbean Sea and Pacific Ocean labeled.]

www.prim-ed.com   Prim-Ed Publishing   Exploring geography: North America   83

North America's forests

Forests are an important natural resource in North America. They provide food and homes for many animals. They also provide the planet with oxygen. When forests are logged, trees can be made into products such as paper, furniture and timber.

Coniferous forests

Coniferous forests cover most of Canada, as well as parts of the western United States. Coniferous trees have cones and needles for leaves. They do not lose their needles in the winter and, for this reason, are sometimes called *evergreens*. Types of coniferous trees include pine, spruce, cedar and fir. Some of the tallest and oldest coniferous trees in the world are the redwoods in northern California. Coniferous forests are logged to produce timber for buildings and for products such as toilet paper, cardboard and printer paper. In Canada, most of the timber is exported for use in the United States.

Deciduous forests

Deciduous forests are found primarily in eastern North America. Deciduous trees have leaves that drop off in autumn. The deciduous trees in the New England region of the US are known for their leaves turning beautiful shades of yellow, orange, brown and red each autumn. Some examples of deciduous trees are oak, maple, beech, chestnut, elm and aspen. Wood from deciduous forests is used to make paper products, timber for building, furniture and musical instruments.

Tropical rainforests

Tropical rainforests are found in Mexico, Central America and on some of the Caribbean islands. It rains a great deal in a tropical rainforest and is hot and humid. This climate creates a fertile environment. There are tens of thousands of different plants and animals in the rainforest. Trees are so crowded that they must compete for sunlight. Most of the trees and plants form a canopy over the rainforest. Some tall trees grow above the canopy to reach the light. The ones that grow below the canopy have broad leaves to absorb as much sunlight as possible. Vines, flowers, ferns and other plants grow everywhere, even on the trees themselves. With over 900 different species of trees, the rainforests in Costa Rica are thought to be some of the world's most diverse.

Rainforests provide important resources. In addition to supplying the planet with oxygen, they are also full of plants that can be used to make medicines. Unfortunately, many of the rainforests are being cleared for timber or to make room for grazing cattle and growing crops. Many rainforest plants and animals have lost their habitats and are endangered or already extinct.

Name _____

Valuable resources

North America's forests

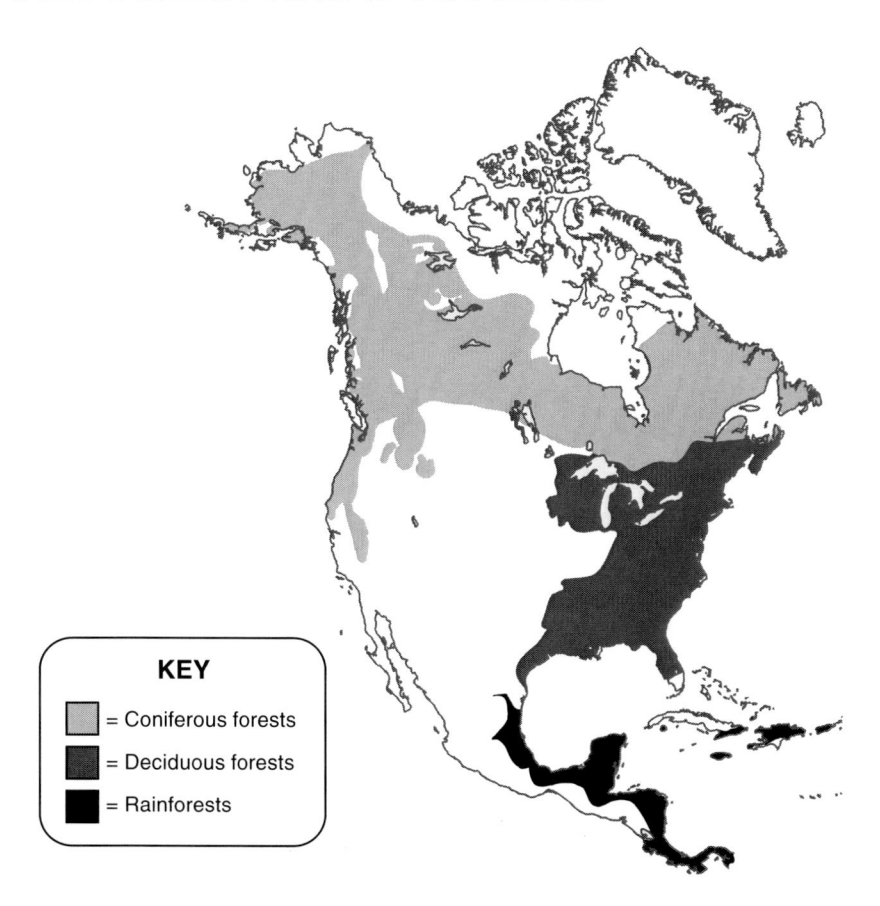

KEY
- = Coniferous forests
- = Deciduous forests
- = Rainforests

Unscramble the word below each line to complete the sentence. Use the information on page 84 to help you.

Some of the answers will need to start with capital letters.

1. Rainforests provide _____ to the planet.
   gonexy

2. Coniferous trees have cones and _____.
   selened

3. Deciduous trees lose their leaves in _____.
   tamunu

4. Examples of _____ trees are pine, cedar and spruce.
   cfoisroneu

5. Plants found in rainforests can be used to make _____.
   dimecinse

6. The trees in _____ turn red, yellow, and orange.
   enw danglen

Wildlife of North America

Polar bear

The polar bear is the world's largest land carnivore, or meat eater.

Habitat
- polar ice cap in the Arctic Circle

Characteristics
- male weighs up to 720 kg
- black skin under white fur absorbs sunlight
- layer of fat keeps the bear warm

Diet
- mostly seals, which the bear sneaks up on by waiting near holes in the ice

Behaviour
- hunts and lives alone
- excellent swimmer

Life cycle
- mates in spring
- mother gives birth to two cubs in snow or ice dens in winter
- cubs live with the mother for several years
- lives 25 to 30 years in the wild

Status
- threatened

Humpback whale

The humpback whale is a baleen whale, meaning it filters food from the water.

Habitat
- migrates up to 50 000 km from the arctic regions in summer to warmer waters in winter

Characteristics
- up to 16 m in length
- black on top with white underbelly
- long, narrow flippers

Diet
- krill, which are small shrimp-like animals

Behaviour
- travel in groups
- can jump completely out of the water

Life cycle
- breeds in warm waters in winter
- mother gives birth to a single calf, which stays with its mother for a year
- lives for about 50 years in the wild

Status
- once endangered from overhunting; still considered a species 'of concern'

Name _____

Valuable resources

Wildlife of North America

Bison

Although bison are often confused with buffalo, they are actually more closely related to cattle.

Habitat
- the Great Plains region of North America in both the US and Canada

Characteristics
- shaggy, dark-brown fur; large heads; and short, curved horns
- adult male weighs up to 900 kg

Diet
- mostly grass and herbs

Behaviour
- live in small bands that often come together to form large herds
- migrate a few hundred kilometres south in winter

Life cycle
- mate in August; males engage in fierce head-butting contests to win their mates
- females usually give birth to a single calf in May

Status
- once near extinction, there are over 450 000 bison today

Beaver

Beavers are the largest rodent in North America.

Habitat
- live in lodges they construct from tree branches in marshes, lakes, ponds and small rivers

Characteristics
- large, strong teeth for gnawing through tree trunks and powerful, paddle-shaped tails for swimming
- thick waterproof fur

Diet
- the soft layer beneath the bark of trees, as well as leaves, twigs and buds

Behaviour
- build dams and lodges
- live in family groups inside the lodge

Life cycle
- mate once a year and produce a litter of about four kits
- kits stay in the lodge for two years
- live about 20 years in the wild

Status
- people hunted beavers for their pelts and the species was almost extinct by 1900; has since recovered

Name _____

Valuable resources

Wildlife of North America

Gila monster

The Gila monster is the only venomous lizard that is native to the United States.

Habitat
- lives in the Mojave, Sonoran, and Chihuahuan deserts in the United States and Mexico

Characteristics
- can reach up to 60 cm in length
- black with pink and yellow markings and black bands around its thick tail

Diet
- uses its venom to kill rats, mice and other small mammals, as well as birds and lizards

Behaviour
- lives in burrows it digs in the sand
- can go for months without food

Life cycle
- female lays 3 to 15 eggs in a hole she digs in the sand
- baby Gilas are about 10 cm long
- lives for about 20 years

Status
- threatened by loss of habitat
- protected in the states of Nevada and Arizona

Quetzal

The name 'quetzal' means 'large, brilliant tail feather'.

Habitat
- tropical rainforests of Central America

Characteristics
- brightly coloured feathers in shades of green, red, and white
- male has tail feathers that are up to 1 m long

Diet
- fruit, worms, frogs, and insects

Behaviour
- poor flyer
- avoids predators such as grey squirrels, hawks, and owls by blending in with its environment

Life cycle
- makes nests in rotted tree stumps
- female lays two or three light-blue eggs
- both parents care for the hatchlings that fly at about three weeks old

Status
- endangered due to habitat loss and hunting of their unique feathers
- do not survive in captivity

Name _____

Valuable resources

Wildlife of North America

A. Write the name of the correct animal to complete each sentence.

1. _____ live in the deserts of the United States and Mexico.

   Quetzals　　　**Bison**　　　**Gila monsters**

2. The _____ is the largest land carnivore.

   polar bear　　　**bison**　　　**quetzal**

3. The _____ has babies that are called kits.

   quetzal　　　**beaver**　　　**humpback whale**

4. The _____ is a venomous carnivore.

   polar bear　　　**Gila monster**　　　**humpback whale**

5. The _____ migrates over 50 000 km each year.

   humpback whale　　　**quetzal**　　　**bison**

6. The _____ eats mostly seals.

   Gila monster　　　**polar bear**　　　**humpback whale**

7. _____ live in the rainforests of Central America.

   Quetzals　　　**Gila monsters**　　　**Beavers**

8. The _____ eats mostly krill.

   bison　　　**Gila monster**　　　**humpback whale**

9. _____ are grazing animals.

   Bison　　　**Beavers**　　　**Polar bears**

10. _____ live together in family groups inside lodges.

    Gila monsters　　　**Beavers**　　　**Quetzals**

B. Which of the six animals is your favourite? Why?

_____

Review

Use words from the box to complete the crossword puzzle.

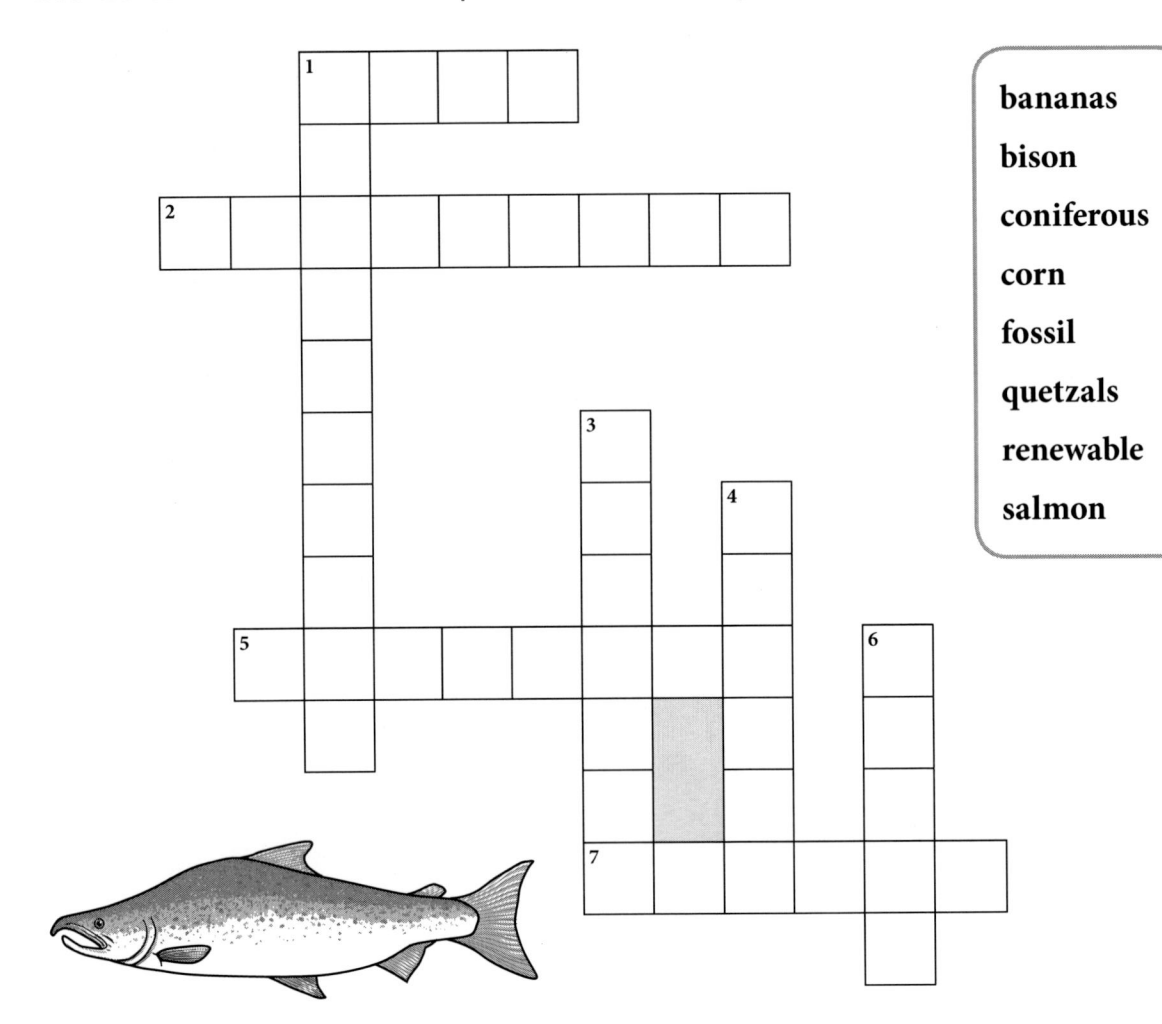

bananas
bison
coniferous
corn
fossil
quetzals
renewable
salmon

Across

1. Most of the US's ____ crop is used to feed livestock.
2. Wind is a ____ resource.
5. ____ live in the Central American rainforest.
7. Today, most ____ are farmed rather than caught in the wild.

Down

1. ____ forests cover most of Canada.
3. Mexico grows nearly 2 million tonnes of ____ each year.
4. Oil, natural gas and coal are ____ fuels.
6. ____ live mostly in the Great Plains region of North America.

SECTION 5

North American culture

This section introduces pupils to the beliefs and traditions of North American people. Pupils learn about cultural influences such as music, art and sports that are important aspects of life in North America. They also learn about different types of North American cuisine and celebrations, as well as religions and native cultures.

CONTENTS

Overview 92–93	Native cultures 104–105
Tourist attractions 94–95	North American cuisine . . . 106–107
Arts and entertainment 96–101	Celebrations 108–109
Religions of North America 102–103	Review 110

Name _____

Culture

Overview

The culture of a group of people is reflected in its customs, traditions and beliefs. One way to learn about a particular culture is to explore its history, celebrations, art and literature. Just as the land of North America is diverse, the culture of the continent differs vastly from region to region.

Tourist attractions

One of the most famous tourist attractions in North America is the Statue of Liberty National Monument in New York Harbour, which includes the Statue of Liberty and Ellis Island, where visitors can learn about immigrants who came to the US. In Mexico, visitors marvel at the ancient Mayan ruins of Chichén Itzá. To the north, tourists can learn about Canadian history at the fortifications, or military buildings, of Quebec.

Arts and entertainment

Many styles of music, including mariachi, reggae and jazz, began in North America. Many famous artists come from North America, as well as some of the world's most loved and respected authors. Another popular form of entertainment in North America is playing or watching sports such as football or baseball.

Major religions

Although the majority of people in North America are Christian, many other religions are observed. Many people come to North America to practise their religion without fear of cruel treatment because of their beliefs.

Native cultures

Many groups of people are native to North America. This means that before any Europeans reached the continent, people were already living there. Native cultures in North America include the Inuit people of Canada, the Tarahumara tribe in Mexico, and the Cherokee people in the United States.

Cuisine

Immigrants who came to North America brought their favourite recipes and cooking methods with them. This has resulted in a wide variety of foods in the United States and Canada. In Mexico and Central America, many dishes include foods such as corn, beans, tomatoes and rice, which were introduced by the Spanish in the 1500s.

Celebrations

In many countries throughout North America, including the United States, Independence Day is an important national holiday. In Mexico, the Day of the Dead is a special holiday to honour those who have died.

Name _____

Culture

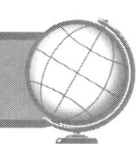

Overview

Tick the box to answer each question.

1. Which of these is *not* a style of music that started in North America?
   - ☐ jazz
   - ☐ polka
   - ☐ reggae
   - ☐ mariachi

2. Which of these is *not* a native culture of North America?
   - ☐ the Tarahumara
   - ☐ the Cherokee
   - ☐ the Inuit
   - ☐ the Irish

3. Which of these is the major religion of North America?
   - ☐ Islam
   - ☐ Buddhism
   - ☐ Judaism
   - ☐ Christianity

4. In which country is the Day of the Dead celebrated?
   - ☐ Mexico
   - ☐ the Bahamas
   - ☐ Canada
   - ☐ Costa Rica

5. Which of these tourist attractions was *not* mentioned as being in North America?
   - ☐ Fortifications of Quebec
   - ☐ Chichén Itzá
   - ☐ Big Ben
   - ☐ Ellis Island

www.prim-ed.com Prim-Ed Publishing   Exploring geography: North America   93

Name _____

Culture

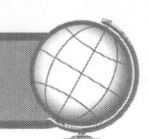

Tourist attractions

There are many interesting landmarks to visit in North America. These sites attract millions of tourists each year who want to learn more about North America's history and culture.

Statue of Liberty and Ellis Island

The Statue of Liberty National Monument is located in New York Harbour, close to both New York City and the state of New Jersey. Visitors come from all over the world to see the famous statue and to visit nearby Ellis Island. Ellis Island is important in the history of the United States. From 1892 to 1954, Ellis Island was the first stop for over 12 million immigrants who wanted to start a new life in the US. As their ships entered the harbour, the new residents saw the Statue of Liberty raising her lamp in welcome. The famous statue, nicknamed Lady Liberty, was a gift from France.

Ellis Island

Chichén Itzá

The ruins of the ancient city of Chichén Itzá are located in the Mexican state of Yucatán. The city was first built by the Mayans in the 6th century. Perhaps the most impressive building in the city is El Castillo (The Castle), a 24-metre-tall pyramid. There are 365 steps on the pyramid, the same as the number of days in a year. Twice a year, on the spring and autumn equinoxes, a shadow cast by the setting sun looks like a snake moving down the stairs. Another fascinating structure of Chichén Itzá is a large court made for playing an ancient game called *tlachtli*. Some researchers believe that losing the game cost the players their lives. The court walls are decorated with sculptures of the winners holding the severed heads of the losers.

Fortifications of Quebec

The city of Quebec in Canada is home to a variety of military structures, including a 4.6 km wall that surrounds part of the city. The fortifications include towers, guard posts, living quarters and the Citadel. The Citadel was a command centre and a stronghold to protect the people in the event of an attack. Thousands of people come to visit the fortifications every year. They can explore ancient-looking towers and turrets. There are also old cannons mounted along the walls, as well as information about how the fortifications were built and used.

Name _____

Culture

Tourist attractions

A. Unscramble the word below each line to complete the sentence. Use the information on page 94 to help you.

Some of the answers will need to start with capital letters.

1. _____ is located in New York Harbour.
   slile dinals

2. Over 12 million _____ came to Ellis Island.
   ramimsting

3. Ellis Island is now part of the Statue of Liberty National _____.
   netommun

4. The ruins of Chichén Itzá are in the country of _____.
   cimoxe

5. Chichén Itzá was founded by the _____.
   anamsy

6. El Castillo was built in the shape of a _____.
   maydrip

7. El Castillo has 365 _____.
   pesst

8. There is a _____ for playing tlachtli at Chichén Itzá.
   rutoc

9. The _____ was a command centre in Quebec.
   tadelic

10. The visitors of the Quebec fortifications can explore _____.
    retrust

B. Which of the three places on the other page would you like to visit the most? Why? Explain your answer.

_____

_____

_____

Name _____

Culture

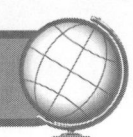

Arts and entertainment

Visual arts

Artist	Fast facts
Ansel Adams 1902–1984	• American photographer known for his black and white photos of nature in the western United States, especially Yosemite National Park
Margaret Bourke-White 1904–1971	• American photographer and photojournalist • first female war correspondent allowed to work in combat zones during World War II
Alexander Calder 1898–1976	• American sculptor who invented the mobile (moving sculpture) • created a miniature mechanical circus
Frida Kahlo 1907–1954	• Mexican painter best known for her bold, brightly coloured self-portraits • married to famous Mexican artist Diego Rivera
Georgia O'Keeffe 1887–1986	• American artist known for her paintings of flowers, bones, rocks and shells • painted landscapes of the south-western United States
Diego Rivera 1886–1957	• Mexican painter famous for his large outdoor murals that often showed historical or political scenes • married to famous Mexican artist Frida Kahlo
Andy Warhol 1928–1987	• American artist who painted realistic images of products such as Campbells® soup cans and Coca-Cola® bottles • painted portraits of celebrities in bright colours

Write the letter of the clue that describes each artist.

(____) 1. Ansel Adams   (a) painted bold self-portraits

(____) 2. Alexander Calder   (b) photographed combat zones

(____) 3. Frida Kahlo   (c) invented the mobile

(____) 4. Georgia O'Keeffe   (d) painted pictures of soup cans

(____) 5. Margaret Bourke-White (e) painted historical and political murals

(____) 6. Andy Warhol   (f) photographed natural places

(____) 7. Diego Rivera   (g) painted flowers, bones, shells, and rocks

Name _____

Culture

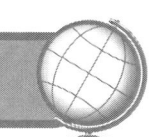

Arts and entertainment

Totem poles

Totem poles are an artform developed by Native Americans on the Pacific coast of the United States and Canada. A totem pole is created by carving figures into a large cedar tree trunk. The figures are usually painted black, white, red, green, green-blue and yellow.

Together, the figures on the totem pole tell a story. The story could be a legend, the history of a family, or a depiction of an important event. In the past, a family member would interpret the symbols on the pole to tell the story.

Poles were also carved to ridicule or shame a person. If a person did not repay a debt, his or her image might be carved upside down on one of the poles and displayed for everyone to see. However, in most cases, totem poles were carved for more positive reasons, such as welcoming visitors or marking the grave of an important person.

Some Native American artists still make totem poles today. They follow traditional methods and do not use modern tools such as chainsaws or electric drills.

Colour the totem pole in the traditional Native American colours mentioned above. Then complete the caption below.

I think this totem pole tells a story about _____

_____

_____

_____

Culture

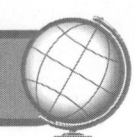

Arts and entertainment

Music

Many different types of music are played throughout North America. Some forms of popular music originated on the continent.

Mariachi

Mariachi is a style of Mexican music that began in the late 1700s. A traditional Mariachi band consisted of musicians playing the guitar, the *vihuela* (a guitar with six sets of double strings), and the *guitarrón* (a large bass guitar). Violins, trumpets and singers were added in later years. Mariachi musicians wear matching suits and large hats called *sombreros*.

Reggae

Reggae got its start in Jamaica in the 1960s and became popular throughout the world. Reggae is a blend of traditional African sounds and rock and roll. Song lyrics usually focus on feelings of social injustice and the challenges of living in poverty. Reggae's most well-known artist is Bob Marley. His music is still popular today.

Bob Marley

Jazz

Jazz got its start in the early 1900s in the southern US. Popular jazz instruments include the trumpet, trombone, bass, piano and saxophone. Over the years, jazz has evolved into many styles, including cool jazz, bebop and jazz fusion. Legendary jazz musicians include Duke Ellington and Miles Davis.

Miles Davis

Circle **yes** if the statement is true or **no** if it is false.

1. Mariachi is a kind of Mexican instrument.	Yes	No
2. A vihuela is a type of guitar.	Yes	No
3. Reggae began in Cuba.	Yes	No
4. Reggae is only popular in the Caribbean.	Yes	No
5. Bebop, jazz fusion and cool jazz are all styles of jazz music.	Yes	No

Name _____

Culture

Arts and entertainment

Literature

North America has produced many famous writers. Even though authors Laura Ingalls Wilder and Maya Angelou were born in different centuries, they both used personal experiences of growing up in North America to write their bestselling books.

Laura Ingalls Wilder

Laura Ingalls Wilder was born in Wisconsin in 1867. She and her family were pioneers in the midwestern United States. While she was still a little girl, Laura's family travelled by covered wagon to Kansas, where they lived for a few years before moving to Minnesota and then the Dakota territory. At age 15, Ingalls became a schoolteacher and taught in a one-room school. She married Almanzo Wilder a few years later.

Later in life, Ingalls began writing about her life as a pioneer in a series of books commonly known as the *Little house* books. The *Little house* books were very popular and are still read by children today. In addition, the books inspired a popular television show about the Ingalls family and life on the prairie.

Maya Angelou

Maya Angelou was born in 1928 in St Louis, Missouri. She spent her early years with her grandmother in the small town of Stamps, Arkansas. The southern states practised segregation at that time and Angelou, an African-American, experienced racial discrimination firsthand. But in Stamps she also experienced the values of faith, family and community, and she learned to love the arts.

At different times in her life, Angelou has been a dancer, singer, actress and teacher of music and drama. But she is best known for her six books that tell of her childhood and early adulthood experiences. The first of these books, *I know why the caged bird sings*, is the most famous. It was made into a television film in 1979. Angelou is also an acclaimed poet. She was asked by President Bill Clinton to compose and read a poem at his inauguration in 1993.

Write two ways that Maya Angelou and Laura Ingalls Wilder are the same. Then write two ways they are different.

Same: _____

_____

Different: _____

_____

Name _____

Culture

Arts and entertainment

Sports

Sports form a big part of life for many people in North America. Children often play on sports teams in their schools or communities. People also watch professional sports.

Americal football and baseball

American football grew out of the English game of rugby. As rules and teams were established, football quickly gained popularity in the United States. Today, most high schools and colleges in the US have football teams. Many people also watch professional football. The 2010 Super Bowl was viewed by over 100 million fans! However, American football is not nearly as popular in other parts of the world.

Baseball is another popular sport in the United States. Although variations of the game have been played for hundreds of years, the first official game was held in 1846 in Hoboken, New Jersey. Within 10 years of the first game, baseball was already being called 'America's national pastime'. Baseball is now a major sport in other parts of North America as well, including Canada, Cuba, Puerto Rico, the Dominican Republic and Mexico.

Ice hockey

Ice hockey is the most popular sport in Canada. Most big cities have ice rinks and professional hockey teams. Every year, Canadian and US teams of the National Hockey League compete for the Stanley Cup.

Canada's greatest hockey star is Wayne Gretzky, who started his professional career at the age of 17. He was the youngest player ever to enter the National Hockey League. Gretzky played with the Edmonton Oilers for nine years, leading them to four Stanley Cup victories. He outscored every other player and won numerous awards. Gretzky retired from the sport in 1999 and was inducted into the Hockey Hall of Fame that same year.

Football

Football is called 'soccer' in the United States, and is more popular in Mexico and Central America. Football had its official start in Mexico on 9 December 1926. Since then, football has grown in popularity throughout the world. Many children and adults play in football leagues and enjoy watching professional matches. Mexico has hosted the World Cup football championship twice.

Name _____

Culture

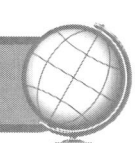

Arts and entertainment

Sports

Using information from page 100, read each clue below and write the correct word on the lines. Then use the numbers to crack the code!

1. Hockey teams in Canada and the United States compete for the ____.

   $\overline{24}$ $\overline{25}$ $\overline{6}$ $\overline{19}$ $\overline{17}$ $\overline{10}$ $\overline{4}$ $\overline{8}$ $\overline{26}$ $\overline{21}$

2. The first official baseball game in the United States was held in ____, New Jersey.

   $\overline{13}$ $\overline{20}$ $\overline{7}$ $\overline{20}$ $\overline{16}$ $\overline{10}$ $\overline{19}$

3. Wayne Gretzky played hockey for the ____ Oilers.

   $\overline{10}$ $\overline{9}$ $\overline{18}$ $\overline{20}$ $\overline{19}$ $\overline{25}$ $\overline{20}$ $\overline{19}$

4. Football is a popular sport in ____ and Central America.

   $\overline{18}$ $\overline{10}$ $\overline{3}$ $\overline{14}$ $\overline{8}$ $\overline{20}$

5. Over 100 million people watched the 2010 ____.

   $\overline{24}$ $\overline{26}$ $\overline{21}$ $\overline{10}$ $\overline{23}$ $\overline{7}$ $\overline{20}$ $\overline{2}$ $\overline{17}$

6. Ice hockey is the most popular sport in ____.

   $\overline{8}$ $\overline{6}$ $\overline{19}$ $\overline{6}$ $\overline{9}$ $\overline{6}$

7. Mexico has hosted the ____ football championship twice.

   $\overline{2}$ $\overline{20}$ $\overline{23}$ $\overline{17}$ $\overline{9}$ $\overline{8}$ $\overline{26}$ $\overline{21}$

Crack the code!

The ____ have won more World Series baseball championships than any other team.

$\overline{19}$ $\overline{10}$ $\overline{2}$ $\overline{4}$ $\overline{20}$ $\overline{23}$ $\overline{16}$ $\overline{4}$ $\overline{6}$ $\overline{19}$ $\overline{16}$ $\overline{10}$ $\overline{10}$ $\overline{24}$

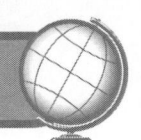

Religions of North America

Christianity

Although many religions are practised in North America, about 86% of the people on the continent are Christian. Most Christians are either Roman Catholic or Protestant. The Protestant faith includes groups such as Methodist, Baptist, Lutheran, Amish and Presbyterian.

Catholic church

People with the same religious beliefs often live in the same area. For example, most of the people who live in Mexico and Central America are Roman Catholic because when Spanish missionaries first came to these countries, they converted many of the native people to Catholicism. There are also many Roman Catholics in north-eastern North America because many Catholic immigrants from Ireland and Italy settled there.

Many religious Christians live in what is frequently called the *Bible Belt* region of the United States. This region stretches across a number of southern and midwestern states. Many of these people belong to Baptist churches.

Two unique Christian groups are the Mormons and the Amish. In Utah, 77% of the people are members of the Church of Jesus Christ of Latter-Day Saints, also known as Mormons. In Pennsylvania, the Amish avoid technology, such as cars or computers, and are known for their plain clothing and skilled furniture making.

Circle the answer that completes each sentence. Use the information above to help you.

1. A person who is _____ is a Protestant.   **Lutheran**   **Catholic**

2. Most Mexicans are _____ .   **Methodist**   **Catholic**

3. In Mexico, _____ missionaries converted many people to Catholicism.   **French**   **Spanish**

4. Catholics from _____ settled in the north-east.   **England**   **Ireland**

5. Many _____ live in the Bible Belt.   **Baptists**   **Amish**

6. About 77% of the population of Utah is _____ .   **Presbyterian**   **Mormon**

7. Many _____ live in Pennsylvania.   **Mormons**   **Amish**

Name _____

Culture

Religions of North America

Other religions

In addition to Christianity, several other religions are practised in North America. These religions include Judaism, Islam, Buddhism, Hinduism and traditional Native American religions. Together, these religions make up about 7% of the population. Just as with Christians, members of these religious groups tend to live in certain areas. For example, 75% of the Jews in Canada live in Toronto and Montreal. In the United States, many Jewish people live in New York and New Jersey. Across northern Canada and Alaska, native people practise the Inuit religion.

Muslim mosque

Although Muslims—people who practise Islam—make up a very small percentage of the population, their numbers are growing. Some of this growth is due to Muslim immigrants coming to North America, and some is due to people who already live in North America converting to Islam.

About 6% of North America's population does not practise any specific religion. This group is also growing. Many young adults report that they are not a part of any religious group.

Use the information above to answer the questions.

1. Name four religions other than Christianity that are practised in North America.

   _____   _____

   _____   _____

2. In what two cities do most of the Jewish people in Canada live?

   _____

3. What are two reasons the Muslim population is increasing in North America?

   _____

   _____

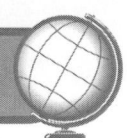

Native cultures

Inuit

The Inuit are a people who originally lived in Alaska and gradually spread throughout the Arctic regions of Canada and Greenland. Because very little vegetation grows in this harsh climate, the traditional Inuit diet consisted almost entirely of meat. The Inuit hunted seals, walrus, caribou, musk oxen and even polar bears. They used the animal hides to make warm clothing and boots called *mukluks*. They also used animal bones and tusks to make tools, hunting weapons and small sculptures. Another animal that became important to the Inuit people was the husky, a dog used to pull sleds over the snow.

The Inuit language is still spoken, and many of the old traditions of hunting and travelling by sled remain. However, the culture has changed because of the influence of modern society. Most Inuit people hold jobs rather than living off the land, and Inuit children are educated in government schools.

Cherokee

The Cherokee are a group of Native American tribes that once lived in the south-eastern United States. Cherokee villages were usually built near a river and included small, mud-plastered cabins and a large council house for meetings. The Cherokee farmed crops that included corn, beans and squash. They also hunted deer, elk and bear for both food and clothing. In the 1800s, the Cherokee developed their own written language and government, called the Cherokee Nation, modelled after the United States government.

In the winter of 1938, the American government forced the Cherokee people to leave their lands and move to land set aside for them in Oklahoma. Today, the Cherokee Nation is a thriving community, blending the old traditions with modern life.

Tarahumara

The Tarahumara live in the Copper Canyon region of northern Mexico. Most still live a traditional lifestyle that does not include modern technology. They live in caves, near cliffs, or in stone or log cabins. They eat a mostly vegetarian diet, growing their own corn, potatoes, squash and beans. They also tend orchards of apples, peaches, papayas and oranges.

The Tarahumara are known throughout the world for their amazing running ability. Villages in Copper Canyon are many kilometres apart, and the terrain is tough for vehicles or even horses, so foot travel is the only means of transportation. Both men and women can run extremely long distances without getting tired. In fact, they often run 80 to 130 kilometres every day! The Tarahumara hunt by simply chasing an animal until it gets too tired to run anymore. They do not wear any special shoes to run. Most run in sandals made from old tyres and leather straps.

Name _____

Culture

Native cultures

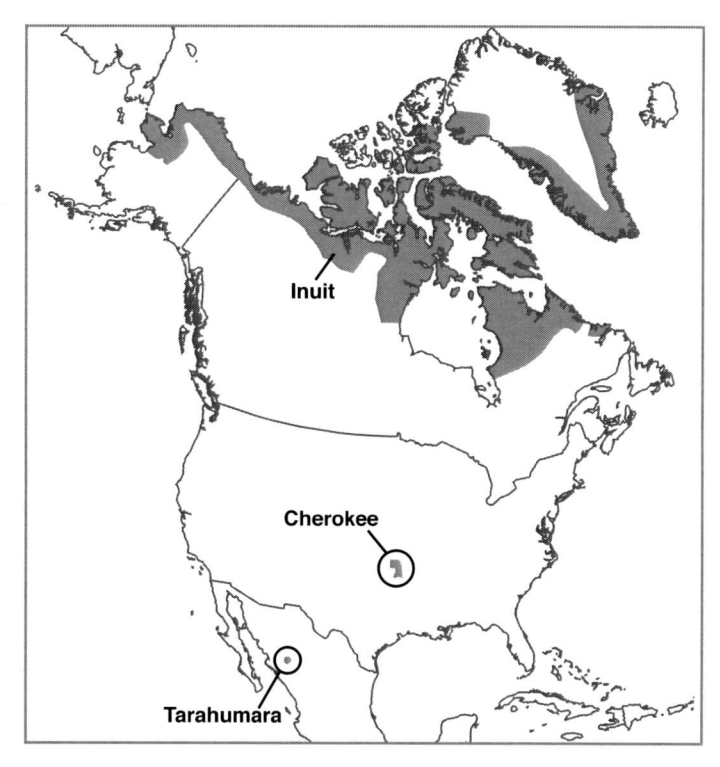

Use the information about the Inuit, the Cherokee and the Tarahumara on page 104 to write two interesting facts about each culture.

Inuit

1. _____

2. _____

Cherokee

1. _____

2. _____

Tarahumara

1. _____

2. _____

Name _____

Culture

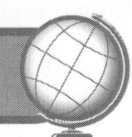

North American cuisine

Mexican cuisine

Mexican cuisine is a combination of traditional native foods and foods that were brought from Spain by early settlers.

In Mexico, corn has been a staple food for thousands of years. Corn is used to make tortillas, which are a part of many traditional Mexican foods such as tacos, enchiladas and tostadas.

Other staple foods are rice, beans and chilli peppers. Rice is often served as a side dish. Beans are often mashed and refried to become part of the main dish or served on the side. Chilli peppers are added to make foods spicy. The most popular pepper is the jalapeño, which is used in many traditional dishes. Chopped up chillies, onions and tomatoes are mixed with spices to make salsa, a sauce that accompanies most Mexican meals.

Chocolate is also used in a wide variety of Mexican foods, from sweet to spicy. In fact, chocolate is a main ingredient in mole (MOH-lay), a sauce that is typically served over chicken.

Caribbean cuisine

Caribbean cuisine contains a blend of several different cultures, including French, Spanish, Indian, African and American. This is because people from so many parts of the world have settled on the islands.

Caribbean dishes often feature the fruits and vegetables native to the tropical climate, such as mangos, bananas, papayas and avocados.

Goat meat is popular on many of the islands. It is frequently made into a stew with dumplings. Another popular dish is called *pelau* or 'cook-up'. To make this dish, the cook uses whatever meats and vegetables are on hand. Pelau is often served with rice or beans. Jerk seasoning is native to Jamaica and popular throughout the Caribbean. Typically, chicken or pork is dry-rubbed with a spice mixture that includes allspice—a type of dried fruit—and a very hot type of pepper.

Seafood is another popular choice in the Caribbean. All kinds of fish are eaten, including shark, crab, lobster and conch, a type of shellfish. In the Bahamas, conch fritters are a favourite.

Name _____

Culture

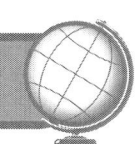

North American cuisine

A. Find and circle the words in the word search. Words may appear across, down or diagonally.

```
A B T Y K H S G T I P A J M
D F S V A E B X O G E U O P
C P C L E U G N S G L B U D
D B H C Z C H I T H A A E E
G E I G A M L S A B U E N I
Z R L C O C A M D E E P C O
Q I L N O S H A A P A O H R
U W I E L T R E X P G V I E
B K E A E I C Q L N M E L T
S N S E B T O P A P A Y A I
R A P D Z N N M A A E V D T
Y C T H R E C W T A S J A U
J P O A I N H B E A N S V K
W O C R C A B A N A N A T L
A M S E N R Z L P O W O T Y
```

banana
beans
chillies
conch
corn
enchilada
mango
papaya
pelau
rice
salsa
tostada

B. In the word box, circle the names of the foods that you have eaten. Then write a sentence about Mexican food and a sentence about Caribbean food.

Mexican food: _____

_____

_____

Caribbean food: _____

_____

_____

Name _____

Culture

Celebrations

Independence Day

Many countries in North America were once ruled by other countries. They celebrate their independence from those countries in different ways. For example, the United States was ruled by Great Britain and declared its independence on 4 July 1776. The US celebrates its Independence Day with picnics, parades, and fireworks. The chart below gives information about other Independence Day celebrations.

Countries	Date	Commemorating independence from ...	Ways of celebrating
Guatemala El Salvador Honduras Nicaragua Costa Rica	15 Sep.	Spain in 1821	To commemorate how the news of independence travelled from Guatemala to Costa Rica, a torch is carried through the five countries, arriving in Costa Rica on the eve of Independence Day. Other celebrations include a paper lantern parade, music and parties.
Haiti	1 Jan.	France in 1804	Haitians eat a special pumpkin soup on Independence Day, which is also New Year's Day. When French colonists enslaved the local population, they would not allow the slaves to eat soup on special occasions. For the Haitian people, eating soup symbolises freedom.
Bahamas	10 July	Great Britain in 1973	People in the Bahamas celebrate the American Fourth of July as well as their own Independence Day, making a week long celebration of parties, picnics and music. The final day ends in a special parade called a *junkanoo*, which features traditional music and elaborate costumes.

Use the information above to help you answer the questions.

1. From what country did Haiti declare independence? _____

2. On what date does Costa Rica celebrate its independence? _____

3. What is a junkanoo?

   _____

4. Why do people in Haiti eat soup on Independence Day?

   _____

   _____

108 Exploring geography: North America   Prim-Ed Publishing www.prim-ed.com

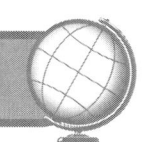

Celebrations

Day of the Dead

The Day of the Dead is celebrated in Mexico on 1 and 2 November. On these days, people remember and honour their ancestors, relatives and friends who have died. Although it might seem that this would be a sad or scary holiday, it is actually a joyous one.

During the Day of the Dead, people visit cemeteries. Graves are cleaned up and decorated with flowers and gifts, including photos, favourite foods and meaningful objects. People often have picnics in the cemetery and, in some parts of Mexico, spend the entire night at the graves of their loved ones. Many people also create shrines in their homes or businesses. These shrines are elaborately decorated with colourful banners; religious items such as crosses and statues of the Virgin Mary; and flowers, candles, food and photos.

During this time, markets are full of toys and sweets made in the shape of skeletons and skulls. People eat sugar skeletons and a special kind of bread called *Pan de Muertos* (Bread of the Dead), which is often shaped as a bun with two 'bones', or long, thin pieces of bread, crossed over the top of it.

Use the information above to complete the paragraph about the Day of the Dead.

People in _____ celebrate the Day of the Dead on the first two days of the month of _____. On these days, people remember those who have died. A common activity is to visit _____ to clean up and decorate grave sites. People also bring food to have _____ in the cemetery and sometimes spend the entire night there. In addition, people create decorative _____ in their homes to honour the dead. During the Day of the Dead celebration, people can buy sweets and toys made in the shape of skulls and _____. People eat a special kind of bread called _____, which means 'Bread of the Dead' in Spanish.

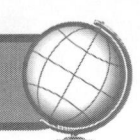

Review

Use words from the box to complete the crossword puzzle.

Word box:
- Haiti
- immigrants
- Mexico
- Mormon
- pelau
- photographer
- reggae
- Stanley

Across

2. Ansel Adams was a famous ____.
4. Many ____ came to the United States by way of Ellis Island.
7. The Day of the Dead is celebrated in ____.
8. ____ is a traditional dish in the Caribbean.

Down

1. ____ is a kind of music that started in Jamaica in the 1960s.
3. People in ____ eat a special kind of soup on Independence Day.
5. Most of the population of Utah is ____.
6. Hockey players in Canada and the US compete for the ____ Cup.

SECTION 6

Assessment

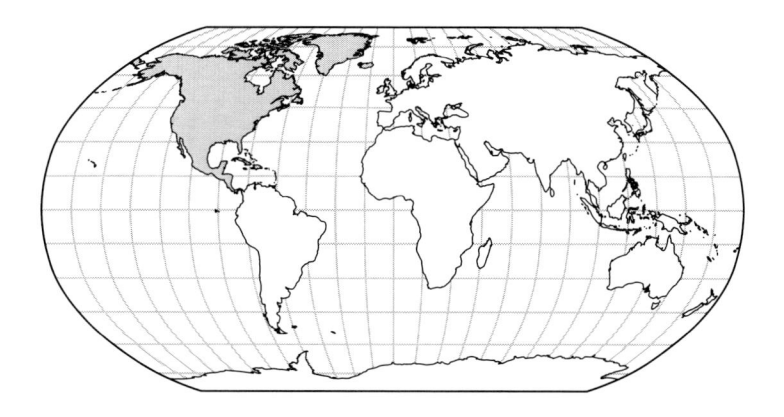

This section provides two cumulative assessments that you can use to evaluate pupils' acquisition of the information presented in this book. The first assessment requires pupils to identify selected cities, countries, landforms and bodies of water on a combined physical and political map. The second assessment is a two-page multiple-choice test covering information from all sections of the book. Use one or both assessments as culminating activities for your class's study of North America.

CONTENTS

Map test. 112   Multiple-choice test 113–114

Name _____

Assessment

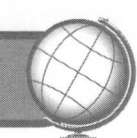

Map test

Write the name of the country, city, landform, river or ocean that matches each number. Use the words in the box to help you.

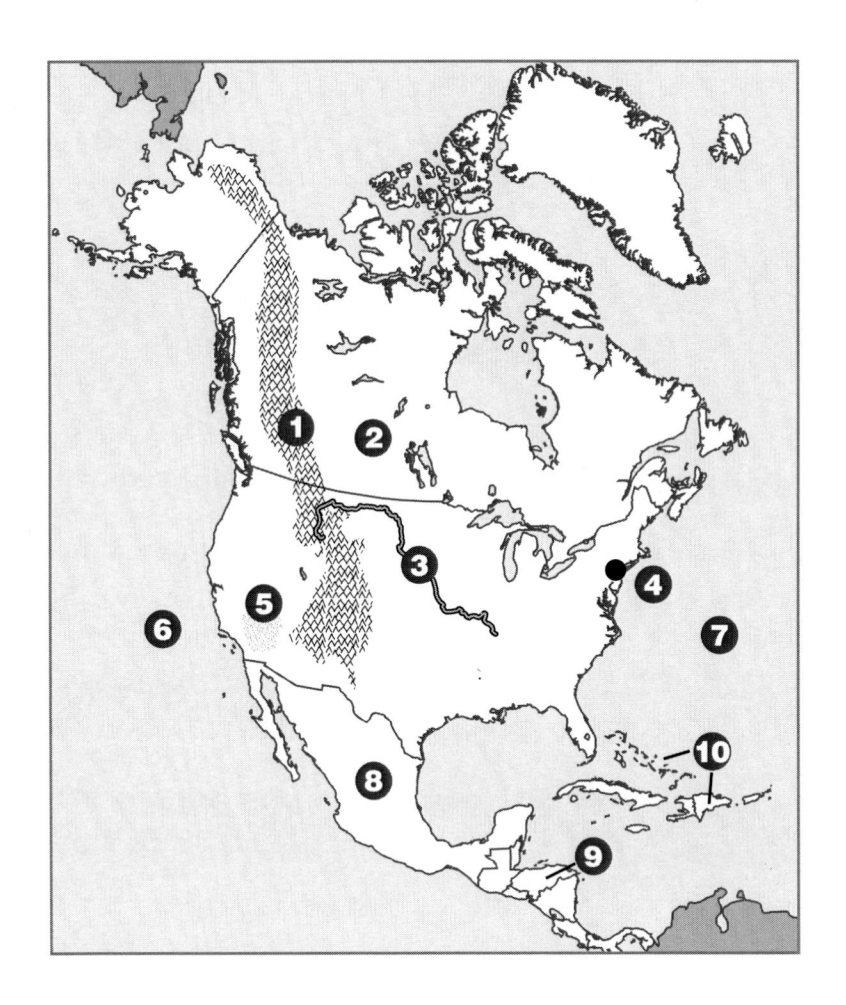

| Mexico | Missouri River | New York City | Pacific Ocean | Rocky Mountains |
| Canada | Honduras | Atlantic Ocean | Mojave Desert | Caribbean Islands |

1. _____
2. _____
3. _____
4. _____
5. _____
6. _____
7. _____
8. _____
9. _____
10. _____

Name _____

Assessment

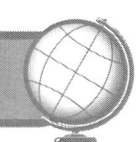

Multiple-choice test

Tick the box to answer each question or complete each sentence.

1. North America is the ____-largest continent in area.
   - ☐ second
   - ☐ third
   - ☐ fourth
   - ☐ fifth

2. Which ocean is east of North America?
   - ☐ Atlantic
   - ☐ Arctic
   - ☐ Pacific
   - ☐ Indian

3. In which two hemispheres is North America located?
   - ☐ Northern and Southern
   - ☐ Eastern and Western
   - ☐ Southern and Western
   - ☐ Northern and Western

4. Which of these is *not* a country in Central America?
   - ☐ Jamaica
   - ☐ Costa Rica
   - ☐ Belize
   - ☐ Guatemala

5. Which one is the tallest mountain in the Rocky Mountain range?
   - ☐ Mount Elbert
   - ☐ Blanca Peak
   - ☐ Mount St Helens
   - ☐ Mount Massive

6. In which two countries are the four major deserts of North America located?
   - ☐ United States and Canada
   - ☐ Mexico and Panama
   - ☐ United States and Mexico
   - ☐ United States and Haiti

7. Which of these is *not* one of the Great Lakes?
   - ☐ Lake Michigan
   - ☐ Lake Erie
   - ☐ Lake Ohio
   - ☐ Lake Superior

8. Which one is the longest river in North America?
   - ☐ Mississippi
   - ☐ Missouri
   - ☐ Colorado
   - ☐ Yukon

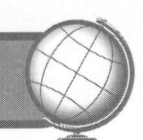

Multiple-choice test

9. Which of these is *not* a renewable resource?
   - ☐ wind
   - ☐ solar power
   - ☐ natural gas
   - ☐ hydropower

10. Most of the corn grown in North America is used to ____.
    - ☐ feed people
    - ☐ feed livestock
    - ☐ make ethanol
    - ☐ make high fructose corn syrup

11. Coniferous forests cover most of ____.
    - ☐ Mexico
    - ☐ Canada
    - ☐ the United States
    - ☐ Panama

12. Where in North America does the Gila monster live?
    - ☐ in the desert
    - ☐ in the rainforest
    - ☐ on the plains
    - ☐ in the mountains

13. Which of these is *not* a North American artist?
    - ☐ Georgia O'Keeffe
    - ☐ Wayne Gretzky
    - ☐ Andy Warhol
    - ☐ Frida Kahlo

14. The main religion in Mexico is ____.
    - ☐ Protestantism
    - ☐ Judaism
    - ☐ Catholicism
    - ☐ Mormonism

15. Which of these groups of people came to Ellis Island between 1892 and 1954?
    - ☐ artists
    - ☐ soldiers
    - ☐ criminals
    - ☐ immigrants

16. What do people in Haiti eat to celebrate Independence Day?
    - ☐ corn
    - ☐ bananas
    - ☐ soup
    - ☐ sweets

SECTION 7

Note-takers

This section provides four note-taker forms that give pupils the opportunity to culminate their study of North America by doing independent research on places or animals of their choice. (Some suggested topics are given below.) Pupils may use printed reference materials or internet sites to gather information on their topics. A cover page is also provided so that pupils may create a booklet of note-takers and any other reproducible pages from the book that you would like pupils to save.

FORMS

Physical feature 116
Suggested topics:
- Appalachian Mountains
- Great Plains
- Gulf of Mexico
- Hudson Bay
- Sierra Madre Mountains

Animal 117
Suggested topics:
- American alligator
- American flamingo
- Bald eagle
- Grey seal
- Mexican wolf

Tourist attraction 118
Suggested topics:
- The Alamo (US)
- British army forts (Bermuda)
- Bonsecours Market (Canada)
- Empire State Building (US)
- Plaza de la Constitución (Mexico)

City 119
Suggested topics:
- Boston, United States
- Kingston, Jamaica
- Puebla, Mexico
- San Francisco, United States
- Toronto, Canada

Cover page 120

Name _____

Physical feature

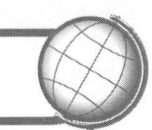

Select a physical feature of North America. Write notes about it to complete each section.

_____
(Name of physical feature)

Location

_____
_____
_____
_____

Interesting facts

_____
_____
_____
_____
_____
_____
_____
_____
_____

Description

_____
_____
_____
_____
_____
_____
_____
_____
_____

Animals or plants

_____
_____
_____
_____

Name _____

Animal

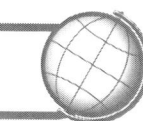

Draw a North American animal. Write notes about it to complete each section.

_____
(Name of animal)

Endangered? (Yes) (No)

Habitat

Physical characteristics

Diet

Behaviours

Enemies/defences

www.prim-ed.com Prim-Ed Publishing

Exploring geography: North America **117**

Name _____

Tourist attraction

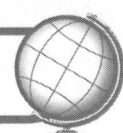

Draw a North American tourist attraction. Write notes about it to complete each section.

_____
(Name of tourist attraction)

Location

_____
_____
_____

Description

_____
_____
_____
_____
_____
_____
_____
_____
_____
_____

Interesting facts

_____
_____
_____
_____

Exploring geography: North America — Prim-Ed Publishing   www.prim-ed.com

Name _____

City

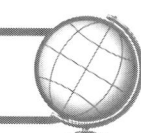

Select a North American city you'd like to visit. Write notes about it to complete each section.

My trip to _____
(Name of city)

Location
_____
_____
_____
_____

How I would get there
_____
_____
_____
_____
_____

Things I would see and do
_____
_____
_____
_____
_____
_____
_____
_____

Foods I would eat
_____
_____
_____
_____
_____

Learning the language
How to say 'hello':
_____

How to say 'goodbye':
_____

Exploring geography: North America

NORTH AMERICA

Answers

Page 7
1. third
2. South America
3. Indian Ocean
4. North America is located in both the Northern and Western hemispheres.
5. the location of a place compared to another place

Page 8
A. Europe, south, Arctic, east, Pacific
B. Teacher check

Page 11
A. 1. (c) 4. (e) 7. (g)
   2. (f) 5. (d) 8. (i)
   3. (h) 6. (b) 9. (a)

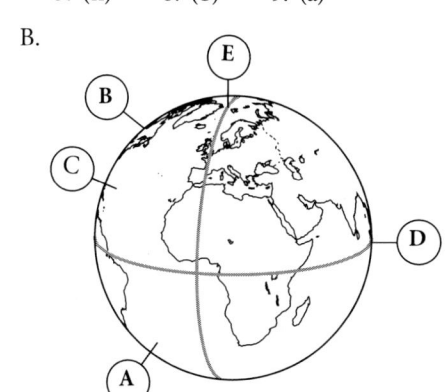

B.

Page 13
A. 1. equator   4. 90°N   7. parallels
   2. prime meridian 5. latitude lines 8. 40°N
   3. 100°W   6. 15 degrees   9. 150°W

B. because North America is in the Northern and Western hemispheres

Page 14
1. No   6. No
2. Yes   7. No
3. No   8. Yes
4. No   9. Yes
5. Yes   10. Yes

Page 16
Across   **Down**
2. projection   1. Atlantic
3. Pacific   4. relative
5. hemisphere   6. equator
7. third   8. Europe

Page 19
1. third
2. 23
3. the United States of America
4. in urban areas
5. Mexico City and New York

Page 20
A. Questions and answers will vary.

Page 21
B. 1. tripled   5. 500
   2. 2050   6. 649
   3. steady   7. two
   4. 220   8. 2050

Page 23
Pupils should colour Canada and Greenland green, the seven countries of Central America orange, the islands of the Caribbean yellow, Mexico red, and the United States blue.

Page 24
A. Answers will vary.

Page 25
B. 1. Canada (colour will vary)
   2. United States (colour will vary)
   3. Mexico (colour will vary)
   4. Nicaragua (colour will vary)
   5. Honduras (colour will vary)

Page 26
A. 1. (f)   6. (j)
   2. (g)   7. (e)
   3. (a)   8. (i)
   4. (h)   9. (b)
   5. (c)   10. (d)

B. 1. 2
   2. 6

Page 27
C. Answers will vary.

Page 28
A. 1. No   6. Yes
   2. Yes   7. No
   3. Yes   8. No
   4. No   9. Yes
   5. No   10. Yes

Page 29
B. Answers will vary.

Page 30
A. regions, capital, Southeast, Hawaii, Alaska, Pacific, territories, Virgin Islands

B. Teacher check.

C. 1. Rocky Mountain
   2. Pacific
   3. Northeast and North-Central
   4. Northeast and Southeast

Page 32
A. Answers will vary.

Answers

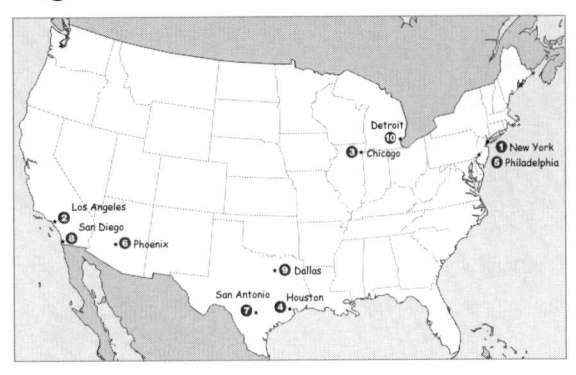

Page 33

Page 34

A. North America, world, 31, Mexico City
B. 1. Jalisco
   2. northwest
   3. Baja California Sur
   4. Coahuila

Page 35

C. Baja California Norte, Sonora, Chihuahua, Coahuila, Nuevo León and Tamaulipas

Page 36

A. **Population**   **Area**
   1. Guatemala   1. Nicaragua
   2. Honduras   2. Honduras
   3. El Salvador 3. Guatemala
   4. Nicaragua   4. Panama
   5. Costa Rica   5. Costa Rica
   6. Panama   6. Belize
   7. Belize   7. El Salvador

Page 37

B. Teacher check.
C. Answers will vary.

Page 38

A. 1. Yes   5. Yes   9. No
   2. Yes   6. Yes   10. No
   3. No   7. No
   4. No   8. Yes

Page 39

B. Pupils should colour Cuba, Jamaica, Haiti, the Dominican Republic and Puerto Rico. Then they should complete the caption. Answers will vary.

Page 41

A. Costa Rica: San José   United States: Washington, DC
   Barbados: Bridgetown   Mexico: Mexico City
   Canada: Ottawa   St Lucia: Castries
   Belize: Belmopan   Nicaragua: Managua
   Cuba: Havana   Jamaica: Kingston
   Bahamas: Nassau   Honduras: Tegucigalpa

B.

Page 42

Across   **Down**
2. Canada   1. capital
7. twenty-three   2. Caribbean
8. population   3. continental
                        4. continent
                        5. seven
                        6. New York

Page 45

1. Denali is in the Rocky Mountains.
2. Sahara
3. Pacific, Atlantic, Arctic
4. 1/5
5. Missouri

Page 46

A. 1. coastal ranges   5. Baffin Island
   2. Sierra Madre ranges   6. Great Basin
   3. Denali   7. Canadian Shield
   4. Great Plains   8. Yucatán Peninsula

B. Pupils should colour the following:
   Yellow: Chihuahuan Desert, Great Basin Desert, Mojave Desert, Sonoran Desert
   Brown: Appalachian Mountains, Coastal Ranges, Rocky Mountains, Sierra Madre Ranges
   Circled in light green: Coastal Plain, Great Plains
   Circled in dark green: Canadian Shield

122   Exploring geography: North America   Prim-Ed Publishing   www.prim-ed.com

Answers

Page 49

1. Yes
2. No
3. Yes
4. No
5. No
6. No
7. Yes
8. Yes
9. No
10. Yes

B.

Rank	Mountain peak	Rank	Mountain peak
1	Mt Elbert	6	Uncompahgre Peak
2	Mt Massive	7	Crestone Peak
3	Mt Harvard	8	Mt Lincoln
4	La Plata Peak	9	Grays Peak
5	Blanca Peak	10	Mt Antero

Page 51

A.
1. Arizona
2. 446 km
3. 1.6 km
4. sandstone, shale, limestone
5. Over millions of years, the Colorado River eroded layers of rock.

B.
1. Answers will vary.
2. Answers will vary.
3. Answers will vary.

Page 53

1. south-west
2. a plant
3. pocket mouse
4. Great Basin
5. Mojave
6. Mojave
7. Sonoran
8. Chihuahuan
9. Great Basin
10. Sonoran

Page 54

A.
1. an environment in which the ground is permanently frozen and no trees can grow
2. an area of land that has coniferous forests; cold, snowy winters; and short, warm summers
3. because it has a harsh climate and is mostly covered in ice

Page 55

B. Teacher check

Page 56

A. Answers will vary but could include:
1. logged for timber
2. cleared to grow crops
3. cleared to create pastures
4. cleared for road construction

Page 57

B.
1. destroyed
2. per cent
3. timber
4. pasture
5. kinds
6. government

Crack the code!: spider monkeys

Page 59

1. volcanoes
2. crust
3. North American
4. Montserrat
5. Six
6. Grenada
7. 1766

Page 60

A. (map labels)
1. Arctic Ocean
2. Atlantic Ocean
3. Pacific Ocean
4. Gulf of Mexico
5. Gulf of California
6. Caribbean Sea
7. Hudson Bay
8. Lake Superior

B.
1. Chukchi Bay
2. Gulf of California
3. Atlantic Ocean
4. Gulf of Alaska
5. Baffin Bay

Page 62

A. Answers will vary.

Page 63

B.
1. Lake Superior
2. Lake Erie
3. Lake Ontario
4. Lake Huron
5. Lake Michigan
6. Lake Superior
7. Lake Ontario
8. Lake Michigan

Answers

Page 64

A. [map of North America with rivers labeled]

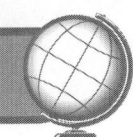

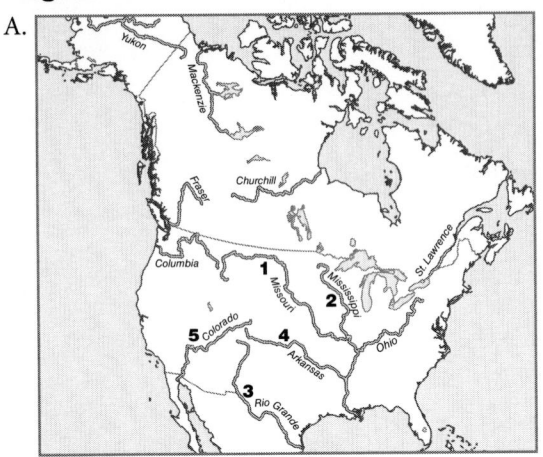

Page 65

B. [word search grid]

Page 67

1. Atlantic
2. wide
3. eleven
4. locks
5. hinges
6. France
7. August
8. Ancon

Page 68

Across
2. Panama Canal
4. erosion
5. Missouri
7. Gulf of Mexico
8. volcanic

Down
1. Lake Superior
3. rainforest
6. tundra

Page 71

1. wind
2. olives
3. coniferous forests
4. Gila monster
5. quetzal

Page 73

A.
1. Yes   6. Yes
2. No   7. Yes
3. No   8. No
4. Yes   9. Yes
5. No   10. Yes

B. 1. Mining coal can be harmful to the environment.
   2. Burning coal causes pollution.

C. 1. eastern
   2. Arctic and Atlantic

Page 75

A. 3, 7, 6, 5, 1, 4, 2

B. Answers will vary, but could include:
1. They make it impossible for fish to swim upstream and lay their eggs.
2. They make the water warmer, which is not good for some plants and animals.
3. They cause a build-up of mud and silt, which can clog a river.

C. Answers will vary, but could include:
1. It is a renewable resource.
2. It is relatively inexpensive to produce.
3. It does not cause much pollution.

Page 77

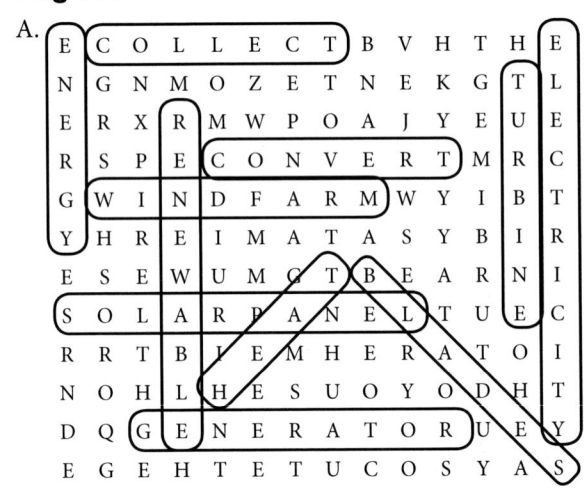

A. [word search grid]

B. Answers will vary.

---

124 Exploring geography: North America Prim-Ed Publishing www.prim-ed.com

Answers

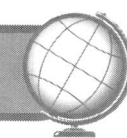

Page 79
A. Answers will vary.
B. 1. North Atlantic Ocean
   2. Canada
   3. pollution, dams and overfishing
   4. They can spread diseases and parasites, and breed with the wild population so their offspring have less of a chance of surviving.

Page 81
1. half
2. corn
3. ethanol
4. feedlots
5. California
6. turkeys

Crack the code!: Holsteins

Page 82
A. 1. over 5 million tonnes
   2. over 700 000 tonnes

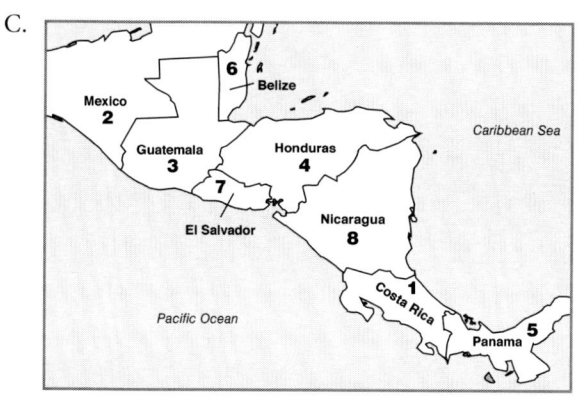

Page 83
B. 1. bananas
   2. highlands
   3. Costa Rica
   4. Guatemala
   5. bananas
   6. coffee

C. [Map of Central America with labels: Mexico 2, Belize 6, Guatemala 3, Honduras 4, El Salvador 7, Nicaragua 8, Costa Rica 1, Panama 5, Caribbean Sea, Pacific Ocean]

Page 85
1. oxygen
2. needles
3. autumn
4. coniferous
5. medicines
6. New England

Page 89
A. 1. Gila monsters
   2. polar bear
   3. beaver
   4. Gila monster
   5. humpback whale
   6. polar bear
   7. Quetzals
   8. humpback whale
   9. Bison
   10. Beavers
B. Answers will vary.

Page 90
Across
1. corn
2. renewable
5. quetzals
7. salmon

Down
1. coniferous
3. bananas
4. fossil
6. bison

Page 93
1. polka
2. the Irish
3. Christianity
4. Mexico
5. Big Ben

Page 95
A. 1. Ellis Island
   2. immigrants
   3. Monument
   4. Mexico
   5. Mayans
   6. pyramid
   7. steps
   8. court
   9. Citadel
   10. turrets
B. Answers will vary.

Page 96
1. (f)   2. (c)   3. (a)   4. (g)   5. (b)   6. (d)   7. (e)

Page 97
Answers will vary.

Page 98
1. No   2. Yes   3. No   4. No   5. Yes

Page 99
Same: They both wrote stories based on their own personal experiences and both were teachers.

Different: Wilder grew up in a family that travelled through the Midwest, while Angelou was raised in the South. Angelou dealt with segregation, while Wilder did not.

Answers

Page 101
1. Stanley Cup
2. Hoboken
3. Edmonton
4. Mexico
5. Super Bowl
6. Canada
7. World Cup

Crack the code!: New York Yankees

Page 102
1. Lutheran
2. Catholic
3. Spanish
4. Ireland
5. Baptists
6. Mormon
7. Amish

Page 103
1. Islam, Judaism, Buddhism, Hinduism
2. Toronto and Montreal
3. There are more Muslim immigrants. Some North American citizens are converting to Islam.

Page 105
Answers will vary.

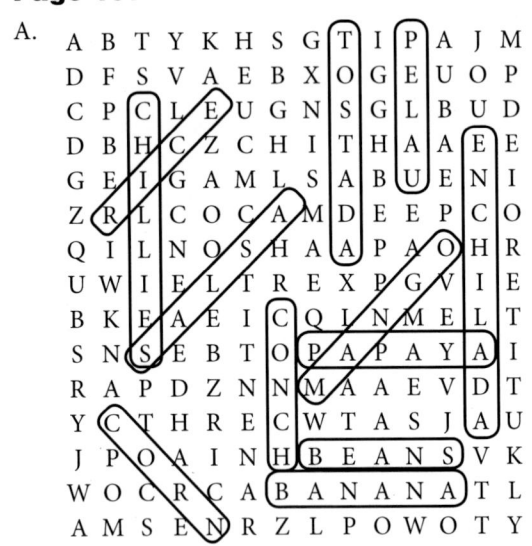

Page 107
A. [word search grid]

B. Answers will vary.

Page 108
1. France
2. 15 September
3. a special parade to celebrate the Bahamas' independence from Great Britain
4. because in the past, French colonists did not allow them to eat soup

Page 109
Mexico, November, cemeteries, picnics, shrines, skeletons, Pan de Muertos

Page 110

Across
2. photographer
4. immigrants
7. Mexico
8. pelau

Down
1. reggae
3. Haiti
5. Mormon
6. Stanley

Page 112
1. Rocky Mountains
2. Canada
3. Missouri River
4. New York City
5. Mojave Desert
6. Pacific Ocean
7. Atlantic Ocean
8. Mexico
9. Honduras
10. Caribbean Islands

Page 113
1. third
2. Atlantic
3. Northern and Western
4. Jamaica
5. Mount Elbert
6. United States and Mexico
7. Lake Ohio
8. Missouri

Page 114
9. natural gas
10. feed livestock
11. Canada
12. in the desert
13. Wayne Gretzky
14. Catholicism
15. immigrants
16. soup